My Heart Will Choose To Say

My Heart Will Choose To Say

A Story of Cancer, Faith and Growing Up

John Musgrave

11 10 09 08 07 06 05   7 6 5 4 3 2 1

First published 2005 by Spring Harvest Publishing Division and
Authentic Media
9 Holdom Avenue, Bletchley, Milton Keynes, MK1 1QR, UK
and 129 Mobilization Drive, Waynesboro, GA 30830-4575, USA
www.authenticmedia.co.uk

British Library Cataloguing in Publication Data

A catalogue record for this book is available
from the British Library

ISBN 1-85078-620-8

Cover design by Stephen Liddell
Print Management by Adare Carwin
Printed and Bound by J. H. Haynes & Co. Ltd., Sparkford

To my 'core support team':
Andy, George, Mark, Ray and Suzie –
without you I wouldn't have made it

Contents

Contents

Acknowledgements

Thanks to Adrian Plass and Alison Hull for both encouraging me to write and helping me shape this book. Thanks to my three families, The Musgrave Mafia, the Welcome Baptist gang, and the awesome Spring Harvest crew, your support has kept me going.

Foreword

There are two things in particular that I like about John Musgrave's book. The first, and most easily underestimated, is that it is a very good read. Worthiness can be unspeakably dull. This account of suffering and hope is far from dull. The very heart and soul (not to mention the body!) of the writer are exposed in such a warm and vulnerable way that the reader is engaged from beginning to end.

The second thing I like is that the book is unswervingly truthful. No doubt this will annoy some people, particularly those who like their Christianity cut and dried and sewn up and tucked safely away where you don't really have to look at it too closely. John has pulled no punches when it comes to talking about the doubt, failure and disappointment that have been part of his experience of dealing with the cancer that has been consuming his body. Nor, thank goodness, has he been any more reticent about his fluctuating, surviving, ultimately upholding awareness of the presence and love of God over the last few years, through music, through ministry and very often through the hands and helpfulness of friends. Following Jesus is a funny old business, as those who have been doing it for a while will tell you, and it is so refreshing to be allowed to view such an honest, granular and warmly engaging reflection of that necessarily vague truth.

I pray that God will speak to you and bless you through the words on these pages.

Adrian Plass
February 2005

1. You are My Rock in Times of Trouble

You are my rock in times of trouble,
You lift me up when I fall down,
All through the storm
Your love is the anchor,
My hope is in you alone.[1]

I can remember the first time I heard the song *Faithful One;* it was at a funeral. I was struck by how much the words so obviously meant to the family who had lost their wife and mother. They were working their way through the storm of bereavement, but still knew where to place their hope. This song is so often sung with determination, out of a desire to state the truth, that we do have somewhere to turn to, to cling to, when storms rage against us. At the funeral as I sang this song, I had no idea that the biggest storm of my life was about to come crashing down.

When I was twenty-one, I went to the doctor because I was regularly bleeding from my back passage. I had some tests and they discovered that I had a polyp which was not cancerous. I was told that if I was older they would probably have removed it to avoid any risk of cancer developing, but that it was not an area of concern for a young man.

I lived with the bleeding which came and went over the next nine years but first went to see my GP when a strange lump developed at the top of my leg in my groin. At first my GP thought it was a hernia, but two months later, as it grew larger, he forwarded my case to a surgeon. I waited on the list for three months but wasn't too concerned. I had told my GP about the bleeding, which by now was constant but I didn't know enough about cancer to be concerned.

I think the surgeon knew something was wrong as soon as he examined me. Within four days I was in hospital. He had discovered a large lump in my back passage and said they would do a biopsy on it and the lump in my groin.

I was scared stiff of hospitals, confused by the large building, many signs and the general hustle. A friend dropped me off at the main entrance but I got so wound up trying to find the ward that I thought I would give the whole thing a miss. Lost in the maze of corridors, I decided I'd rather go home but unfortunately couldn't find the exit either. Somehow I stumbled into the right ward. Before I knew it I was in a bed, wearing a horrible gown and strange stockings, awaiting my trip to the operation room.

I knew I was going to be put to sleep but that was about all. I didn't know what a biopsy meant and fully expected to be out of the place by the end of the day, having been told there was nothing to worry about. Things did not go as I expected. The day dragged on; 'nil by mouth' – including water – was a new and unpleasant experience. The waiting, being unsure of what was going to happen and when, only served to add to my dislike of hospitals. Eventually my time came and I was wheeled down to surgery. I hadn't expected to go into a proper operating room. I realise now how naive I was, and how unprepared. I was put to sleep and woke some time later in the recovery room, drowsy and freezing cold. Blankets were piled on me and I fell back to sleep, waking later on the ward. The fact that something serious had taken place came as much as a shock to me as it did to my parents, who arrived to find me white as a sheet and clearly not in good health.

The decision had been made to remove both lumps. On venturing under the sheet to see what had been going on, I discovered I'd been shaved in places unshaved before and I had a large nasty looking scar. I was covered in yellow gunge and it all looked rather horrific. Still, I comforted myself with the thought that it was better to get it all over and done with in one go.

I'm not designed for hospital wards. I slept badly; every bleeper, ringing phone and groan from recovering patients kept me awake. I made the mistake of trying to go to the loo on my own, unaware of what the odd shaped cardboard thing by my bed was for. The walk opened the wound and I had to be helped back to bed. The loss of dignity hit hard as I was so unprepared. During the following day I wondered if everybody else had been given a manual, telling them what to come to hospital with and what to expect. Everybody else seemed to know what to do. When told to have a wash I was at a loss what to do. I'd been told not to get out of bed and didn't want a repeat of the night before's unpleasantness. I felt like a naughty school boy when the nurse returned and asked why I hadn't washed. Timidly I asked where I should wash and was told they would get me a basin of water. She seemed actually cross that I didn't have any wash things and looked at me as if I was mad when I explained I didn't come expecting to stay overnight. I imagine that if everything hadn't been so sudden it would have been explained to me what was going to happen and how to prepare but there just wasn't the time.

My friend Mark came to rescue me. I was aware that having had a general anaesthetic, I couldn't go home alone. Mark, having had his own medical dramas, was far more aware of how things worked in hospitals. Knowing the ward secretary, he sweet-talked her into speeding up my discharge, found me a wheelchair and we made our escape. I am eternally grateful for Mark's excitement at all things medical. Without his enthusiasm I would have overdosed on the various pills I was given, totally unable to listen to any of the instructions accompanying them. He got me home and into bed, and delivered me into the hands of my family when I was a bit more comfortable and able to face the drive to London.

It took me a few weeks to recover. It seemed that I had lost my body's thermostat as I was constantly switching from being too hot to being freezing cold. My sleep patterns were all out of sync. I woke up really early every day but needed to go back to sleep after being up an hour or so. It felt like I slept more than I was awake. I think other people, more aware of medical matters, had begun to expect there could be more to the sudden operation and removal of these lumps. I, however, being totally ignorant of what cancer really was and how it operated, didn't suspect anything sinister. Even as the date for my visit to the surgeon to discuss findings drew near, I didn't feel worried or have any feelings of dread. It wasn't until I got a letter asking me to bring my parents to the con- sultancy meeting that I felt something was wrong. They wouldn't be asking a thirty-year-old to bring someone with him unless something of importance was going to be said. I don't normally panic but fear filled me. Once again Mark's inside knowledge of the NHS was of value as he phoned the hospital. He was unable to get more information but did manage to get my surgeon to bring forward the day of the meeting to the next day, Friday, rather than the following Monday. Despite everyone saying it was probably routine to have someone with you, I knew then something was wrong.

Being told I had an aggressive cancerous tumour in my bowel was a far more calm and orderly event than one would expect. Having watched *ER* and *Casualty* you would expect more drama! My surgeon spoke clearly, explaining that I had a tumour which had spread through the bowel wall into the surrounding muscle. The accessible part in my back passage had been removed in the operation. The lump in my groin had been a swollen lymph gland, to which the cancer had also spread; this also had been removed. I can't remember all that was said but I clearly remember him saying that this was a serious situation, that I had a long battle ahead that would involve chemotherapy and radiotherapy, but that I should focus on the end result. He said that I had a 20 per cent chance of surviving the cancer but that I should focus on that 20 per cent chance, not the 80 per cent chance that the cancer would spread and finish me off.

It all felt totally unreal, as if they were talking about somebody else. I felt numb and unable to respond emotionally. I have experienced the same feeling many times since and I can't quite explain it. It's not that everything around you stops, although things do seem to go a bit slower. You seem to glide through it in a daze. Things happening to you, horrible things that you know should upset you, don't seem to have an effect. Things that should shock and bring fear don't seem to register. Yet under it all, at some subconscious level, you know things aren't right and it hurts.

As we sat in that room, I struggled to remain focused on the conversation. At one point the surgeon expressed concern that I lived alone and I realised that they were talking about the possibility of me moving back in with my parents in London. The feeling of losing control over my life did hit me at that point. I was not ready to make any big decisions but I knew clearly that I wanted my work, social, church and home life to stay as they were, and to keep my independence. I didn't panic about being told that I had cancer and could lose my physical life, but I panicked to think I could lose *my life*. I was angry that the conversation was turning to treatments and practicalities when the reality was hard enough to accept.

Emotions have a funny way of breaking through the numbness of these situations in unexpected ways. Only once with the surgeon did I cry, but only a little. It wasn't until I had to tell someone over the phone that any pain surfaced. I struggled to get the words out, feeling unbelievably confused and hurt. However, it passed. My parents and I went up onto the South Downs for a walk and we all focused on being normal, and strangely it wasn't that hard. Later they went home and my friends came round. Despite some tears we mainly had an enjoyable evening. We got a take-away curry, steered the conversation to happier things and somehow on the surface things were fine. I was still recovering from the op and experiencing moments of sudden tiredness and so my friends literally put me to bed and left. I fell asleep but soon after they were gone woke again. I felt crushed by an emotional pain, not a physical one. I couldn't hold back the tears. Despite all the support I had received that day I felt incredibly lonely, lost, and God seemed a long way away.

I did sleep again and woke feeling surprisingly calm. Much of the following day was spent on the phone calling friends. I wanted those close to me to hear first from me. It was hard telling people, knowing what I was saying would ruin their day. The unreality of the situation helped as I didn't feel I was talking about me. In a strange way it felt like acting. I spent the day with my friend George. When together we both seem to encourage each other's practical characteristics, not the emotional ones. She helped me work through the phone calls before putting on a video. The day passed peacefully.

That evening I headed off to spend the evening with my friend Rachel. While for most of the day I had felt in control I was scared that as soon as I was alone again, I would experience the crushing hurt of the night before. I decided to avoid being alone. I was frightened, scared by the emotions that seemed to be simmering underneath, unsure of where they were coming from. I suppose I expected people who had been told bad news to react in one of many different ways. Some would break down, cry and be unable to control their emotions. Others would go into denial and grimly refuse to accept the facts. Some would feel numb and unable to respond. Others would be able to get on with things. I didn't realise that you could experience more than one response and found that I went through a number of different reactions. I could easily switch between being grimly determined not to give in and then despair. I set off, feeling calm and halfway through my journey I had to pull over as the tears were blocking my eyes, making it hard to see. I knew Rachel had a few friends round for the evening and couldn't face turning up in such a state. I called Andy, my pastor, and ended up at his house.

I hadn't been going to Andy's church for very long but we'd got to know each other a bit over a few pub lunches and he knew me quite well at that point. He was wise enough and kind enough to let me cry, not to tell me everything would be okay. I wish I could remember all that we spoke about that evening but I know it had a deep impact on me. Up to that point I had not spoken about what was going on inside to anyone. I hadn't dared face the fact that I could be dying of cancer and that my life was about to change dramatically.

The people I had been with had been focusing on getting me through those few days and encouraging me not to feel despair. What I felt inside, though, had to come out. On a rational level I wasn't able to accept the facts, but on an emotional level something hurt so much that it couldn't be held in. Andy helped me realise that it was okay to let this hurt out, to cry, to feel despair. I know somewhere in that conversation he acknowledged the fact that I could die. It felt so good for someone else to say it, to face it, not to feel I was the only one who was thinking about it. I also know that at some point I said I wasn't sure if I wanted to go on living. This wasn't based purely on the present circumstances. For a few months before the diagnosis I had been trying to tackle some of the things in my life that caused me grief; the demons in the cupboard that were stopping me living my life to the full. I had decided to face up to, not run away from, things in my personality and character that needed to change. At that point the cancer seemed too hard to cope with, on top of the other things I was trying to deal with. I realised that I could hide behind this cancer, let everybody love me and support me through it and forget about the other things and maybe death would even be a release. I only briefly entertained such thoughts but for a short period of time during that conversation, death seemed to be an easier way out.

Then God quietly stepped into that conversation. I didn't hear a voice. I didn't fall over in the Spirit and God didn't give a word of prophecy to Andy but, as we talked, God began to make it clear to me that he existed, that he loved me, cared about what was happening to me and that he was in control. My feelings changed from wanting to die to definitely wanting to live. I wanted to face all my problems and issues, I wanted to beat cancer, and I wanted to become a stronger and better person. I didn't stop crying, in fact I went to Rachel's house and we spent most of the night crying together. I didn't stop hurting, but from that point on I knew that God was very definitely real and very much with me in what was happening.

* * *

I need to take a step back, to tell you of my past, to try and explain who I was before that point. I grew up in a Christian family and was part of a lively church. I can't remember a time when I did not know about God and feel love towards him. At University I took Religious Studies as part of my Bachelor of Education course. This challenged many of my beliefs and taught me to be brave in asking questions about mine and other people's faiths. I didn't lose my faith but began to question it, and didn't find it easy to accept much of what I heard preached in the churches I went to. Growing up, Christianity seemed quite straightforward, the Bible told you what was what, you believed it and did your best to put it into practice. University showed me the diversity not only of religious expression but of beliefs and attitudes within the Christian faith.

For the next few years I had times when I knew God closely, felt him directing my life and caring for me. I enjoyed worshipping God whenever I could. I also experienced times when I doubted not God's existence, but that he was the God taught to me by the church. I rarely enjoyed a sermon and struggled to come to any firm description of what I truly believed and understood. After a short period of teaching I joined a mission with the intention of spending a few years teaching children of missionaries. I was to go and teach in a mission school in the now Democratic Republic of Congo. Before I left the missionaries were withdrawn because of political instability. I ended up in Paris learning French in preparation for joining a team on the Comores Islands where I home-tutored some MKs, as they are known in the trade. I was to stay for two years but things didn't quite go to plan and I ended up back in the UK six months later.

My understanding of how the Christian faith worked was severely challenged. I thought that if you had a willing heart, God was able to use you; and that if you were willing to serve God overseas, then your Christian life was sure to grow. Great things would happen. You would see success and find happiness. I knew that you would have to face hardship, but somehow I believed your faith would go from strength to strength, questions would be answered and doubts fade. This hadn't been my experience. I had tried to step out and serve God but the two years of mission service had been full of changed plans, confusion, disappointment and failure. I felt I had many more unanswered questions, lots more doubts, and a much weaker faith.

After returning to the UK I did some supply teaching but hated it and wanted to try something different from teaching. It's hardly surprising that a few months' supply teaching in London would put someone off teaching, but it was more than a case of being put off. I was searching for a place where I could fit, feel useful, and maybe even be of value to God. By chance, I ended up temping in the head offices of Spring Harvest during the 1999 event. Spring Harvest is a large interdenominational Christian conference which takes place over the Easter holidays with an office of full-time staff who work throughout the year planning the event. While the full-time staff set off to the various sites to run the conference, I remained in the office answering phones and replying to emails. I got on well and for the first time ever actually enjoyed going to work. I was offered a permanent job and began working on the Word Alive week of Spring Harvest and then another conference called At Work Together. I loved it. I felt I fitted in and knew roughly what I was doing. The head office was based in Sussex, an area of England I have always loved and wanted to live in. I found somewhere to lodge in a village not far from the office and made new friends. Life had turned for the good.

Spring Harvest is managed by a group of people called the Spring Harvest Leadership Team. When I first met them at the office, Jeff Lucas, one of the team, said something that clicked and made me realise I was with like-minded people. He said that he had stood on the Big Top Stage, faced four thousand people and doubted the very existence of God, wondering if all of the activity around him was some kind of mass delusion. When he said that, I felt I fitted; if he had such doubts then it surely was okay for me to have them too. I have since learnt that I'm not alone, apparently nearly all Christians have periods of doubt, where they wonder if God exists at all. I grew up in church, I knew people had doubts, I just didn't know it was okay to have them.

For a few years I was a Christian nomad, drifting from church to church, not because I wanted to go but because I felt I had to. I finally found a local church where the people seemed friendly and someone always talked to you. I enjoyed the worship, even the teaching but it was the Pastor who insisted on standing at the only exit from the premises to say 'Hello' that finally pegged me down. For years the end of a church service was the bit I hated the most. It was the bit that made me feel that I didn't fit, shouldn't really be there. I had too many questions and doubts to be a good church member. Normally I could quietly slip away after only the one embarrassing conversation where I told someone else I worked for Spring Harvest, had moved down from London, wasn't married and didn't have children. At the Welcome Baptist church the Pastor at the gate proved an additional hurdle. There didn't even seem to be a back fence to jump over!

Eventually I took up his offer to chat and told him what I tell you now. Despite my Christian heritage, despite being a missionary, despite organising a truly awesome Christian event, I wasn't a great Christian full of strong faith living a powerful life for God. I was confused, doubtful, forever living on the fence, unable to decide what I truly believed. I couldn't fully accept God nor walk away from him and I was disappointed with much of my life.

Why am I telling you this? Because I know how to play the game. I could present my story and make it all sound wonderfully easy. I could be the good Christian young man who out of his strong faith turned to God in his time of trouble, knowing he was safe. Of course he felt God's presence, of course his faith gave him strength and a hope, why wouldn't it? Of course he was healed, he knew who to turn to and his faith made him whole. I could give easy answers; those who believe in God and faithfully serve him will be healed. I could throw in some verses and tie it neatly up with God as great and powerful, and me as the Christian hero. But it just wasn't like that!

When God showed up on that night, one day after I heard that I had cancer, I experienced something I had never before fully experienced, the reality of God's existence. To a person who struggled daily with his faith, he said 'I'm real' and 'I'm here.'

My storm had only just started but there was my rock, my hope. I cried out to God, as the song says, again and again, and there he was, and I felt safe.

Note

1 Brian Doerksen *Faithful One* (©1989 Vineyard Songs Canada, admin by Copycare)

2. It is Well with My Soul

When peace like a river attendeth my way
When sorrows like sea billows roll
Whatever my lot Thou has taught me to say
It is well, it is well with my soul.[1]

I am not someone who easily says that it is well with my soul. I have had to be taught. I have seen people who are totally filled with God's peace. For some I'm sure they were born with a peaceful disposition and so a peaceful state comes more naturally, yet I imagine from time to time that peace is tried. For most people, I imagine peace isn't their natural state. I think you can't claim it, you can't force yourself to be peaceful, but you can learn to be and can be taught.

Peace did not come with the knowledge of God's reality. I didn't float gracefully through the days that followed. My first Sunday at church was anything but graceful. The church was told and they had a time of prayer. People I didn't really know prayed loving and powerful prayers. It was not these that made me cry. I sat listening, still unable to accept that it was me they were talking about, praying for. I couldn't have cancer. Despite this inability to accept the facts I couldn't hold back the tears. I didn't understand the pain that rose and took complete hold of me and I didn't know where it came from. I was unable to keep things together no matter how

I tried. I managed to pull myself together after the time of prayer but lost it when I tried to join the congregation singing *How Great Thou Art*. I couldn't get the words out and something totally broke inside me. I couldn't feel God close to me, he didn't feel very great at that moment. I have never cried or been as hurt as I was at that moment. I literally wanted to curl up in a ball on the floor. I didn't understand where these emotions were coming from but could not calm myself down. Andy pushed his way down the aisle behind me and threw his arms over my shoulders and held me. It felt like I was being held together, that without his arms I would crumble to the floor. I could well have ended up rolling on the carpet, I needed someone else to hold me up. And there was God again. He wasn't going to let me fall apart and be crushed by circumstances, he wasn't going to let me be alone. He was there, right there in the pit of despair that had engulfed me. Again, no words, no manifestations of power. He worked through his children, a guy willing to hold his friend together physically and emotionally, surrounded on each side by friends who were not edging away in embarrassment, and a congregation able to carry on singing one of the greatest hymns ever written.

I've cried in public before. I'm someone who doesn't try that hard to hide it but I still struggle with the masculine ideal of not being seen to cry. I don't understand my tear ducts at all. Show me a horrible scene on the news, not a drop. Tell me something terrible, nothing. Yet when I'm in a difficult situation, feeling low or just plain tired, they flow all too easily. I wish I could control them better, shed a quiet tear at the right moment, and keep a stiff upper lip at others. However, that Sunday it was different, and even now I don't quite understand what was going on inside me. I do know that I learnt a few lessons during that service. The first is let people cry.

Rarely does good come from trying to hold in all of your emotions. Secondly, it's okay. Somehow along the winding path of my Christian life I had picked up the idea that Christians shouldn't feel depressed, they shouldn't despair, for isn't God in heaven and in control of everything? Yes, but Jesus wept over Lazarus, and he must have known he was about to raise him from the dead! He didn't stop the lady from using her tears to wipe his feet even though he knew he was about to forgive her sins. I'm not suggesting that Christians live in permanent defeat or forget what God has done. But there are times when darkness and despair take over and to pretend it's not happening or put on a forced show of victory when your heart is breaking is not what God requires. God can meet you in many ways at that dark moment, he can hold you, even if you feel like you are about to break.

The tears took well over a week to stop properly and they seemed ready to fall at any moment. I cried when the youth group came and prayed for me at the end of the service, yet that was a powerful moment when I felt amazingly supported. I went into work and told the guys in the Monday morning prayer session and lasted only a few moments before being overwhelmed. The sea billows kept rolling in. There were lulls between but no fair weather. I managed to hold the tears off throughout my first set of scans, a CAT and MRI. As I sat drinking the foul liquid they give you before the CAT scan I was beginning to realise that hospitals, appointments, waiting rooms and stupid gowns that tie up the back and leave nothing to the imagination were going to be the norm, now and maybe for a long time into the future. Yet through that first week, God's reality and love continued to surround me.

He worked through my friend Rachel who supported me, giving me a place to stay when I couldn't face being on my own. She was willing to travel with me on the new and scary journey. She cried with me when I needed to cry but also let me laugh and be happy when the clouds moved a little. We spent hours talking things through. We were able to talk about God and my new found sense of his reality. We began tentatively to give the situation to God, asking him to use what lay ahead to change us for the better. We looked into the Bible to see what he had to say. We dared to ask for healing, but deeper than that, that he would change us. God worked through Andy who guided me through the first day of scans, keeping my mind off things when needed, being there to listen when I needed to talk. There were times of humour mixed in with the sadness. We had quite a laugh when we realised that the Macmillan nurse misheard my introduction of Andy as my Pastor. I'll let you guess what she thought our relationship to one another was! When it was all over, he let me cry and anointed my head with oil and prayed for my healing, again drawing the situation back to God. I now have such a better understanding of what is meant by the church being the body of Christ; 'God with skin on' as I've heard it described.

* * *

You shine[2]

At the end of the first week I woke up feeling low. I felt drained by the emotions of the week, a bit sore from having stitches out and a bit freaked out by the new experiences of CAT and MRI scans. Throughout the week kind people had been sending me cards full of care and support. The verses sent did bring encouragement and I began to appreciate the Bible in a deeper way. One friend sent me a tape, *You Shine* by Brian Doerksen. I wasn't quite in the mood for Christian music but decided to settle in the lounge with a cup of tea, expecting to drift off after a few songs. The first one struck an instant chord.

> In this world we will have trouble
> But You have overcome the world
> You shine
> Brighter than the brightest star
> Your love
> Purer than the purest heart
> You shine
> Filling us with courage and strength
> To follow You.

The words were incredibly clear and relevant to how I was feeling, yet pointed to a truth that I needed to focus on. God had not promised a life without trouble, but he had overcome all troubles, his love was pure and he filled us with courage and strength. These words allowed me to feel pain, and didn't pretend that my situation was irrelevant in the light of all of God's amazing plans. However, they were showing me that God had something to say about it, and that even amidst the pain it was still right to praise God.

Each song had something to say to me.

> I am convinced
> No force on earth
> Can separate us
> From the love of God
>
> Angels or demons
> This life or death...

Violence or danger
Hunger or shame
Won't separate us
From the love of God.[3]

I was beginning to understand a little how cancer could change my life for ever and eventually claim it, yet it was not a force powerful enough to separate me from God.

I had not heard the next song before but I could identify with it so easily at that point.

I don't know what this day will bring
Will it be disappointing
Or filled with longed for things

I don't know what tomorrow holds
Still I know I can trust Your faithfulness

I don't know how or when I'll die
Will it be a thief
Or will I have a chance to say good-bye

I don't know how much time is left
But in the end I will know Your faithfulness

When darkness overwhelms my soul
When thoughts are storms of doubt
Still I trust You are always faithful
always faithful[4]

I am so grateful that some songwriters are brave enough to write songs expressing the darker side of our emotions. These words were not overriding my emotions, they were giving them validity. It was okay to feel as I was feeling, it was okay to think about my death as something other than a glorious step to heaven. More importantly, I was not failing when the darkness overwhelmed me, even at that point I could still trust God.

Many of the songs were taken from the Psalms. I found strength in the fact that even writers of the Bible struggled and battled with fears that God had forsaken them.

How long oh Lord will You forget me
How long oh Lord
Will You look the other way

How long oh Lord
Must I wrestle with my thoughts
And every day
Have such sorrow in my heart

Look on me and answer
Oh God my Father
Bring light to my darkness
Before they see me fall

But I trust in Your unfailing love
Yes my heart will rejoice
Still I sing of Your unfailing love
You have been good
You will be good to me.[5]

How better to learn Scripture than to put it to music? I sang this and let the truth sink in. I was not alone in feeling confused and hurt, I was not alone wrestling with my thoughts, or calling on God to answer. I was in good company! David, who wrote this Psalm, knew times of immense trial but he knew where to place his trust. The word that burns out of this song is *but*. Despite doubts, unanswered questions, sorrow and pain, we can and should trust in God. God had been good to me, throughout my whole life I have seen his goodness to me in so many ways, and this goodness would be seen again, cancer or no cancer.

The next hymn I had forgotten but it soon came back to me and I could join in, for listening to that tape had brought me to a place where the words were now true. *It is well.* I couldn't sing the words of this hymn and truly mean them until I had been taught a few lessons. Firstly, I was not exempt as a Christian from pain and suffering. Secondly, my feelings of doubt, despair, fear and pain were genuine, and God accepted them as such. Thirdly, God was with me through all of it. I needed to believe that and remember that his love was unfailing. Then the peace was able to come and I could say *It is well with my soul.*

The dark times were not over and a lot of challenges lay ahead but at the end of that first week, living with cancer, I had learnt some amazing lessons and been given some tools to face the future. A God who had seemed distant and uninterested in me had suddenly made himself truly known. I also realised that God was going to use this situation for his glory. I had prayed to God and said that he could break me down but begged that he would rebuild me better than before. Even if I was to die young, I pleaded with God that before I died, I would know that he had made me into the person he wanted me to be. Even as I prayed that prayer, I knew he was already beginning to answer it.

Notes

1 J P Bliss and Horatio Spafford, *It Is Well*
2 Brian Doerksen, *You Shine* (© 2001 Integrity's Hosanna! Music/ Sovereign Music UK)

3 Brenton Brown and Brian Doerksen, *I Am Convinced* (© 2002 Integrity's Hosanna! Music/Sovereign Music UK and Mercy Vineyard Publishing/Copycare)

4 Brian Doerksen, *Your Faithfulness* (© 2002 Integrity's Hosanna! Music/Sovereign Music UK)

5 Brian Doerksen, Steve Mitchinson, Karen Mitchinson and Daphne Rademaker, *Psalm 13* (© 2002 Integrity's Hosanna! Music/ Sovereign Music UK), italics mine

3. I'm taking a Sick Day[1]

It wasn't only Christian worship music that left an impression. My friend George has a wonderful knack for finding a song to match every mood. She made me a CD full of songs which put their finger exactly on how I was feeling at certain points or highlighted bits of my character. This song often brought a smile to my face for in the weeks to come I was to take many a sick day.

I had appointments every day bar two for the next two weeks and, apart from a week's break at Christmas, I was to have at least one appointment a week, more than one on most, for the next six months. I quickly had to overcome my fear of hospitals. I certainly learnt my way around Eastbourne District Hospital rapidly finding the short cuts, knowing where to find parking spaces. I also soon became acquainted with many waiting rooms. Only the most saintly of characters can sit in a hospital waiting room for an appointment, which is always late, without grumbling a little. No matter how many times I told myself that the NHS was overworked and that the staff were doing their best, I couldn't help getting wound up as the clock ticked away. The most well padded of waiting-room chairs became impossible to sit on comfortably. The book that I had been wanting to read for ages but couldn't find the time became incredibly dull. No magazine remained glossy enough. I couldn't even manage to nod off and catch up on some sleep. I wished I was anywhere but there. I'm sure others can identify with these feelings. To sit in a waiting room every day didn't do my frustration levels any good. I may have smiled to myself, singing along with 'I'm taking a sick day, I claim this day for me,' en route to the hospital but an hour in a waiting room later, I was wishing I was at my desk.

As far as work was concerned, this couldn't have come at a worse time for me. For over a year I had been working on the Spring Harvest At Work Together conference. This conference focused on Christianity in the workplace. The teaching centred on what God had to say about our work life and how we could serve him in every part of our daily life. The conference was held at the beginning of November in Eastbourne. I was the programme administrator and enjoyed being at the centre of the planning. September and October were to be the exciting months of final preparation. My work days would be busy and challenging; maybe stressful, but definitely exciting. However, instead of being right at the centre I was barely in the office and eventually some of my responsibilities had to be passed over to others. My job title was 'At Work Together Project Administrator'. I jokingly renamed myself the 'Not Very Often At Work Project Administrator'. That changed to the 'Not Very Often Together At Work Project Administrator' after a few tears in the staff-room. Joking aside, I felt I was losing control of my life and became increasingly frustrated.

I suddenly had a new priority in my life which overrode everything else. My oncologist would have signed me off work there and then and I could have walked away from the office and focused entirely on the important job of fighting this life-threatening disease. Nobody would have judged me for giving up work, even at the critical stage before the conference. Looking at the big picture, work was no longer of the greatest importance, nor were any of my other ambitions, hopes and dreams. Everything had to take second place. I couldn't make the switch in my mind. Work was more important at that point than treatment. I couldn't lay aside my goals, my ambitions. Thankfully, this is not a new phenomenon for the medical professionals who understood and did their best to work with my schedules. They didn't put the pressure on me to stop work but the appointments had to continue.

This makes me sound like a workaholic but I'm not. George's choice of first song on my CD was *Lazy* by Xpress. It was my theme song. At any other point in my working life I probably would have quickly placed work a lot further down my priority list. It was more than not wanting to give up. I wanted to achieve something that had eluded me before in my various jobs: satisfaction. Despite some success in my working life, a sense of real satisfaction in what I was doing had always been just out of reach. I wanted to succeed by playing my part in the planning of the conference to the best of my abilities. I had been involved in planning for the main Spring Harvest Event for the previous two years but this conference gave me the chance to put a lot of what I had learnt into practice and to be involved at a higher and broader level than before. Part of me wanted to prove to others, but much more so to myself, that I could be the best at what I was doing. I could reach excellence, I could find satisfaction. Despite remaining involved as much as possible right up to the conference, I felt the opportunity to find that satisfaction was snatched from me because of circumstances completely out of my, or anybody else's, control.

For all of October I struggled with feelings of failure. I felt as if everything I had ever tried to do had come to nothing. I wondered if it was ever worth setting goals, because it never seemed possible to achieve them completely. While on one level it all felt incredibly unfair, I couldn't blame God and didn't get angry with him. Instead, I was angry with me and blamed myself for getting cancer. I doubt this makes sense but I felt in some way I had brought this on myself. I was born on Friday the 13th and I began to wonder if there was any truth in the superstition of bad luck associated with that day. I couldn't focus on the successes of my life or the many things I was blessed with. In those darker moments all I could see were the negative things in my life leading up to that point.

God was still making his reality known to me during this time. Through the care of friends, through song, through verses given to me, he was letting me know he was there and in control. Many times I cried out to him in those weeks, with prayers wrapped in frustration. I asked that if I had to have cancer, would he help me readjust my life and take away the disappointment I was feeling. I asked for a peace that would blot out my feelings of failure. He never gave me what I wanted, but he had a purpose to all of it.

He did help me though. Strangely, work, while at times being a source of frustration, also became a hiding place where I could forget about cancer and focus on something else. Spring Harvest's head office is a great place to work. We have a lot of fun and sometimes I wonder how anything gets done between the joking around. The concern, the care and the love shown to me when I was diagnosed blew me away. I had offers of help from every direction. Everybody was very flexible with me. The only person who ever commented as I broke every working time regulation, dress code and countless other rules was me. People took over my workload but allowed me to remain involved. What was so special, and a lifesaver, was that everyone allowed me to be normal. While there was always someone to talk to and cry with when needed, when I just wanted to be normal, they let me. I carried on working when I could and nobody commented what time I arrived or left. I didn't have to spend hours telling people how I was coping, I could go straight to my desk, turn on my computer and get working. I was included in the office gossip, the jokes, the moans, all that makes up office life. I loved it and found comfort in the normality.

* * *

Lord I can dream of an ordinary life
Where nothing particularly weird is going down[2]

Of course most of my life wasn't particularly ordinary at that point. In fact, my life could have made a good story line in a soap opera. As news spread about my cancer, I became a bit of a celebrity. Maybe that's an exaggeration but suddenly a lot of people knew my name and a fair bit about me. At my church where I was only really known to a few people, suddenly everyone knew who I was.

Through the Spring Harvest network, my home church back in London, and the various people with links to my family, many people suddenly were aware of what was going on in my life. I received many letters, the phone wouldn't stop ringing, I was engulfed in support. In many ways it was amazing to have such support and the value of so much prayer I'm sure was immeasurable. However, part of me struggled with the loss of privacy and wanted to stay well out of the limelight. I would have given anything to turn back time and return to my relative anonymity.

If cancer wasn't enough of a story line for my soap opera lifestyle, I had a few more unusual things happen around me. I had recently bought my own flat. The sale and move had been relatively straightforward. I was extremely surprised when the bailiffs turned up on my doorstep looking for the previous owner who, having sold up, had skipped the country avoiding debts. Phone calls had to be made to separate myself from him, and I learnt some more about dealing with solicitors, debt collectors and estate agents.

The drama didn't stop there. While trying to rest at home one afternoon, I was drawn into a strange incident in my street. A lady living across the road had pulled a gun on two of her visitors. Both had made a run for it and hidden in the lobby outside my front door. I was unsure what to do but when I saw a police car pass I thought I would investigate. As I walked out of my drive I managed to stumble between the police who had blocked the road with their car and were pointing their guns down the street, and the lady from across the road who was now waving her gun back at them. The police shouted for me to get back inside and I obeyed without question. I had just got back in my flat when one of the people who was hiding banged on my door. I opened the door on the chain to find a very distressed lady, begging to be let in. She had been hiding under our stairs! I did the English thing and made her a cup of tea. Out of the window I saw the police leading the gun woman away, so felt safe to go and bring a police officer to the lady. This is a very brief description of the tale, there's more to it and it's all bizarre. I could write a chapter, but I'll cut it short by saying the lady with the gun had previously been a male member of the SAS!

A few days later, I was contemplating how much had happened in a short period of time. So much drama. I was sitting in the waiting room of an infertility clinic, a place I never expected to enter before marriage. Being on the verge of starting chemotherapy and radiotherapy, I had been warned that the treatment could make me infertile and it would be good to take some precautionary measures in case I wanted children in the future and was unable to father them. At first I sat there, surrounded by pictures of happy parents and newborns and shook my head in disbelief. This couldn't be real. How could the events of the past few weeks have happened? At first I was angry; why did this have to happen to me, how could this be right, fair, what God wanted for me? Then I realised that I had a lot going for me. I had cancer but hundreds of people were willing to support me. I had not felt the need to take my hurt and pain out on anyone else. The value of Christian faith was beginning to show. In times of trouble, help would come. In difficult times there could still be normality, friends, jokes and even work. I understood that God was holding me up.

I understand now that people go through situations that make my life look like a pleasant stroll in the park. I'm aware that people suffer greatly and have to deal with a lot of pain. I hope the fact that God held me up through my trials won't bring pain to people who are going through their own trials and to whom God seems so distant. Yet I'm compelled to give a testimony, God did help me through my trials.

* * *

I won't be made useless, won't be idle with despair[3]

Chemotherapy is a word which brings fear to many people. It's associated with being horribly sick, hair loss, tiredness and many other nasty side effects. It's one of those dreadful medicines that often makes you feel more ill than the actual sickness it is trying to combat. The many different drugs have different side effects and people's bodies respond in different ways. In the chemotherapy ward I saw those who were suffering greatly. I can only thank God that I managed almost six full months on various chemotherapy drugs but suffered very few side effects. I didn't lose my hair and was only once actually sick. I am extremely grateful not to have had to suffer. A recent story line in the medical drama *ER* focused on a young boy dying of testicular cancer, made bald, weak and sick by chemotherapy. I could identify with his sentiments that he was too young to have this illness. I was about thirty years younger than the average bowel cancer patient. I could understand the terminology as much the same had been said to me. I realised, though, how different my experiences were to his. I hadn't suffered that much and I'm still so grateful.

* * *

If I could tell the world just one thing
It would be we're all okay
Not to worry because worry is useless in
times like these.[4]

This song by Jewel pretty much sums up my attitude before starting chemotherapy. I felt it was useless to worry. I had to have it. I was more nervous than scared of the possible side effects. This was partly because of my continual inability to believe that this was really happening. Also, there was no point in fretting in the face of a bigger enemy, the cancer.

I had a PICC line fitted. It was a tube which entered my arm and ran into a vein. Through this, blood could be taken and the chemotherapy drugs pumped in. Rachel deserves a medal for sitting with me as they used a needle with a hole big enough to pass the tube through. She bravely remained, only turning a little pale when blood spurted across the room. From my point of view it wasn't too bad, as I had a local anaesthetic cream and couldn't see what was going on because of the position they had me in. I had to have my head turned to one side so that, as they fed the tube into the vein, it went down towards the heart and not up towards the brain. To this tube was fitted a strange pump which fed the chemotherapy drugs into me continually. It was called a pump but this doesn't explain it properly. It was a tube inside which was a balloon full of the drugs. I wore this pump for a week and my blood pressure naturally drew the drugs into the vein. Over the week the balloon shrank and once a week I was fitted with a new pump. It was extremely odd having tubes coming out of my arms and this strange pump hanging from my belt. It drew a few comments, some of the ruder variety, but generally went unnoticed.

For a few days after I started the chemotherapy, I woke feeling a bit sick. Generally a glass of water and a dry biscuit did the trick. I had to adjust my activities a little. I found that if I overdid it, I could suddenly feel faint and sick, but soon learnt my limits. I was glad I hadn't sunk into despair at the thought of chemotherapy as it wasn't too bad. The difficulty lay in trying not to get any of the equipment wet. I had to text Rachel 'Come quick, bring Marigolds' when she came to dinner as I realised I hadn't washed up anything for weeks. Washing myself was an even greater problem but this was solved by a friend from work buying me vets' gloves, the type that cover your whole arm and are used to examine cows' insides. They did the trick.

Unfortunately, after only a week I began to get pains in my arms and by the time I went to my second chemotherapy appointment to get the pump changed, the pains had spread across my shoulders. I was feeling weak and finding it difficult to stay on top of things. The line had become infected and had to be removed. I was kept in hospital for four days.

The chemotherapy ward was a much nicer ward than the surgical ward I'd first stayed on. It was quieter and the staff were really lovely. There was a day room where people came for blood transfusions and various chemotherapy treatments, and two small wards. The doctors and nurses whom I saw for regular treatment were around, so it felt less threatening. Sadly this happened over the weekend of my thirtieth birthday. It was extremely gutting to mark this milestone in hospital. I was allowed out for a few hours on my birthday but it was horrible waking up on the day being on the ward. The nurse who came to take my blood pressure and feed me pills asked for my date of birth, as they normally do. I nearly cried when he didn't realise that the day was my birthday. Thankfully, friends and family made up for it as soon as visiting hours began.

I nearly gave into despair over that weekend. The stay in hospital brought home to me the seriousness of the situation. Its impact on what was to be my special weekend made me feel that I would for ever be giving up special things. Something stubborn in me, however, wouldn't let me give in totally to despair. I realised that despite all the warnings of what chemotherapy could do, which have to be given to prepare you, and despite the consequences of taking serious medication, I could fight back and win some of the battles. I didn't have to be made useless by despair. Sometimes despair had overpowered me, but other times I felt I had a choice and could fight it. I didn't have to put on a brave face, I could cope and in many ways my life could still be normal.

I met other people on those wards who were facing things much worse than me, but they didn't give in. In fact it's amazing how calmly people came in and were plugged into the machines. The chemotherapy wards and day room were peaceful, and rather like the atmosphere in the lounge of an old people's home. I learnt something about the British stiff upper lip in that ward. It's not about ignoring despair, but there is a value in fighting it at times, and the more you win the battles, the easier it is to face the next challenge.

Notes

1 Cameron Wilson, Daisycutters, *Sick Day* (Mushroom Music)

2 Dan Wilson, Semisonic, *Ordinary Life* (Semidelicious Music, 2001)

3 Jewel, *Hands* (EMI Music Publishing, 1994) "Hands" Words and Music by Patrick Leonard and Jewel Kilcher © 1998, Bumyamaki Music/EMI April Music Inc/Wiggly Tooth Music, USA

4 Jewel, *Hands* (EMI Music Publishing, 1994) "Hands" Words and Music by Patrick Leonard and Jewel Kilcher © 1998, Bumyamaki Music/EMI April Music Inc/Wiggly Tooth Music, USA

4. I'll be There for You[1]

I am an extremely well cared for young man. The support shown to me throughout my treatment was amazing. My parents wanted to take me home when I was diagnosed. They wanted me back, they wanted to care for me. I know that my decision to stay in Sussex was hard for them, but I know they understood why I wanted to stay in my own home and went along with my decision. What made it easier for them to get back in their car and return to London, time and time again, was the strong caring of those around me.

My close friends provided different kinds of support, all of which I needed. I have asked for their permission to include them in this book because they have been as much a part of the story as I have. I wanted to include them here, not just in an acknowledgement and thanks section, but because I learnt some important truths about friendship as they were willing to travel with me.

Rachel provided the emotional back up I needed. She not only was with me at my low points but she helped share the burden by crying and laughing with me. It seems incredibly selfish to want someone to share your pain but I realise now how much I needed someone to show me that what I was going through was hurting them too, yet they weren't going to walk away. I wasn't alone. She was, however, no soft touch and remains one of the few people brave enough to tell me off. At times it feels that we disagree as much as we agree and I know I frustrate her at times, pushing our friendship to the limit. Yet, maybe a bit grudgingly, I know I need keeping in line a bit.

Mark's purpose in life is not really to keep me on the straight and narrow! Despite attempting to be accountable to each other, we are more likely to lead each other astray. If Mark and I were in the same class at school, the teacher certainly wouldn't allow us to sit next to each other. At my request, Mark has been my mentor in the fine art of beer appreciation, taking my education very seriously. He rescued me from my girlie drinking habits, preferring cider and alcopops to the good manly pint. I now have enough knowledge to walk into a pub, select a suitable beverage, and even return it if it not up to scratch. He is far more practical than me and so a great person to turn to when the car won't start. I have already mentioned that he understands the mysterious world of the NHS and has guided me down endless corridors to various appointments.

When I need to talk boy stuff, Mark is there. When I don't want to talk about my emotions, just want to have my mind diverted, he's always willing to head off down the pub for a pint. He's happy to agree with me when something is just plain rubbish but doesn't need to dwell on it and is happy to talk instead about the more important matters of girls and cars.

When I need practical support, he's there sorting me out. When I need someone to defend me, he'll fight for me. Mark and I can and do talk on a deep level, but there are times when you just need to be a bit more shallow and steer well clear of emotions and Mark helps me do that. He has an amazing ability to calm me down. When I couldn't sleep and would lay awake lost in hurt feelings he'd be the one I could turn to and call. He didn't come round for a counselling session. He'd turn up, any time of night and stay with me. The strange thing was that knowing he was on his way always broke the mood I was in. By the time he arrived with his sleeping bag and toothbrush, I'd have pulled myself together. We'd have a cup of tea, maybe a glass or two of port if needed, pray and then I'd go back to bed and he'd kip down on the sofa. I don't know why but when he was there, no matter what state I was in before he arrived, I'd sleep like a baby. I have many male and female friendships and all are valuable, but there is something really valuable in having a mate of the same gender as you, who thinks like you and is there for you.

I'm sure it's time to make George a girl's name as I don't know any male Georges but quite a few Georginas who prefer George. George is my unpaid shrink, able to help me put things into the wider context. Our conversations encouraged me, not to override my emotions, but also not to let them cloud the bigger picture. She's practical and can solve problems. We both share a desire to be efficient at what we do, although she wins on all fronts. Together we make quite a good fighting team, as the members of the housegroup which we both attend can testify to! We both can argue a point, give a balanced view, and we don't stand for too much nonsense. She is a truly great friend.

In addition to these close friendships I have been guided and supported continually by my Pastor and friend, Andy. His advice has again and again been spot on as I have turned to him in need. He has protected me, counselled me, and shown me love way beyond the call of pastoral duty. I'm so grateful that God put me under such a good shepherd.

I could go on and on naming people who have been there for me. My employers, for being willing to put my physical and emotional needs above the needs of work, even if they had to do my work for me. My colleagues who were willing to take me as I am, on a daily basis. My church family, who prayed continually. My family, for loving me, and for my parents, hurt so deeply and unable to protect me but always being there.

This isn't intended to be a tear jerking Oscar prize-winner's speech. I learnt something through this support. I now understand why Jesus calls the church his body and how he works through his children. Through the different types of support my friends and family have offered me, I have felt God's love, care and protecting hand. He didn't step in and heal my cancer after the first prayer. Nor, when showing me his reality, did he physically come into my world. Yet through the amazing support of friends, he provided practical, emotional, and physical strength as well as wisdom and guidance. I have also brought these people to your attention to say 'Thank you.' As the *Friends* theme tune goes, when the rain started to fall, they were there for me. They could have walked away but chose to stand by me, even if it meant sacrifice. I know God will reward them for everything they did for me.

* * *

Some days I hate everything, everyone and everything.[2]

How can I choose such a title to follow the previous sections? I want this book to show the dark as well as the light. This song is about a boy living with parents who are arguing and breaking up. They were trying to hide from him what was going on. I identify with the line 'Please don't tell me everything is wonderful now.'

As time passed, things seemed to settle around me. I had a new line fitted and this one went into my chest and was less likely to get infected. My chemotherapy pump was fitted again and life on treatment fell into a routine, with weekly blood tests and chemotherapy pump changes. Those around me took their cue from me. I wanted life to be as normal as possible and so people treated me normally. While people were willing to ask how I was getting on, generally things quietened and my cancer wasn't the central topic of conversation. I got to the stage where I was happy to be on my own and didn't need anyone with me overnight.

I was able to drive myself to appointments. On a good day this was exactly what I wanted and everything was fine. I didn't want a fuss made over me. I didn't want to have continually to repeat how I was feeling. I didn't want the drama. This, however, could easily change and there were blacker days also, where things were not okay; everything was far from wonderful. I could maintain an appearance of everything being fine but inside I battled with a whole variety of thoughts and fears.

I began to allow doubts into my mind. I questioned whether people really cared. I wondered if people were getting used to me having cancer and that it didn't hurt as much any more for them. Were they thinking that I was well supported, had God on my side and so should just get on with it? Were the strong emotions felt when I was diagnosed receding? Were they getting on with their lives? It hurt to think that people were able to do so when I couldn't get on with mine. It hurt that they maybe were coping while I was still having to fight every day. Things weren't settling down for me. I wasn't getting used to having cancer.

These thoughts, at times, got darker still. I would wonder what it would be like after I died. I knew people would grieve but I would question how long it would be before they found they could get on with their lives again. How long would it be before they could be happy? How long before they forgot me? I misread conversations and responses. I read between the lines 'Everything will be wonderful some day.' I began to think that people preferred to focus on everything being wonderful because it was easier for them, easier than facing the harsh realities of cancer. I wondered if they were just believing I was going to be healed and were happy to sit back and not think too much about it until God got on with it. At times, I felt people were brushing over my emotions because they were no longer having strong emotional responses to my situation. Deeper still, I questioned if they were telling me, not in words but in their actions, that everything would be wonderful one day because for them it would be. I could die but for them life would go on and be fine.

I began to get angry with how people were reacting to me. I didn't let it show but inside it boiled. I found comfort in the lines at the end of this song. The music takes on a more heavy metal tone and the singer shouts out 'I don't want to hear you say everything will be wonderful some day. Some days I hate everything, everyone and everything.' That's how I felt. Some days I was fine, on others I hated everything and everyone. I would drive my car as fast as I could down country lanes with the music blaring out. I'd imagine scenarios where I would crash the car into a tree or maybe get stopped by the police, something dramatic that would force people to react. They wouldn't be able to say 'Everything will be wonderful' because that clearly wouldn't be the case.

These paragraphs may come as a shock to the people who lived around me during those months. On the surface it may have looked as if I was coping well. And I was. For the majority of days I was getting on with my life the best I could and enjoying it. The treatment was not as bad as expected and I was avoiding many side effects. I hope it makes sense when I say that what people saw of me was true and not a mask to cover up the dark things going on in my head. The happy John who could raise his hands in worship despite the tubes trailing down his arms was as real as the John who drove down country lanes considering smashing his car and himself to bits. I, like everyone else, had good times and bad.

I've learnt something while trying to understand my darker moods. Firstly, people don't always react to me in the way I want them to. I wanted people to shape their reactions to fit my moods. If I was happy, then I wanted them to be happy around me. If I was sad, then I wanted them to be sad. Of course, they had to guess my mood, I wasn't willing to tell them. But people aren't like that. They do not always react as I want them to and fundamentally they are not on this earth to make my lot easier and my ride more comfortable. This was a hard lesson to learn.

I had cancer, so shouldn't they have put my needs above their own? No. I'm not saying people shouldn't put other people's needs before their own. I'm saying people shouldn't expect others to put their own needs first. When we sit back and say people should be doing this or that for us, we so easily become bitter and selfish. Yes, accept other people's love and care, but don't expect it or demand it. Instead, when in a position of accepting, be always looking how you can give.

Secondly, I learnt that life did go on without me. After the initial shock of John Musgrave getting cancer, life in Sussex did not grind to a halt. People got on with their lives. While many people prayed for me daily and were genuinely hurt, they still went to work, did the shopping, walked the dog. They had times when they were happy and, shock horror, even forgot the name John Musgrave. I hope you realise that I'm mocking myself, not others. I had to face the hard reality that life would go on without me once I died. My death would not stop someone else living and enjoying their life. My good friend Lisbeth was brave enough to tell me that while she hated the thought of me dying, her life would go on. She would live a happy life and not one in which she mourned me daily. She wasn't being heartless. She told me things in an email about how she would miss me that made me weep and made me realise the place I had in many people's hearts. She was telling the truth, though; her life did not depend on my existence.

There is also a spiritual truth I had to learn. I wasn't 'the one'. The universe was not designed to revolve round me, but designed to revolve around another. Leonard Sweet, an American cultural analyst, says he starts each day by looking in the mirror and saying 'You are not the one.' In a world that is becoming increasingly egocentric, where magazines promote ways in which we can find fulfilment, satisfaction, and our own happiness, we can so easily believe life is all about us and our needs. With all the support and attention I was receiving I was in danger of believing I was the one, the most important, my needs were to come first. Others should look after me before themselves. I learnt, a bit painfully, that I was not to be the central focus of other people's lives. That place belonged to God.

Thirdly, I discovered that having cancer is a lonely experience. For all the support and love in the world, it is still you that has to go to every examination, every appointment. It's you that has to have the treatment and experience the side effects. It's you who ultimately has to survive it or die from it. I know my parents would have taken the cancer from me and died rather than let me suffer. They couldn't do it. Only John Musgrave could be the John Musgrave who had bowel cancer. When I longed for people to show me their emotions, to show me how hurt they were, how hard it was to get through each day with the reality of me having cancer, I was longing for someone to experience what I was going through and make me feel less lonely. It isn't possible, no matter how close a person is to you. Ultimately I was the central character in this particular drama and it was, at times, a lonely role.

These three lessons were valuable but there was a greater lesson to learn, one which took time to understand.

> Before the throne of God above
> I have a strong, a perfect plea
> A great High Priest whose name is love
> Whoever lives and pleads for me.
>
> My name is graven on His hands
> My name is written on His heart
> I know that while in heaven He stands
> No tongue can bid me thence depart.[3]

One of the great mysteries of Christianity is that while we are not 'the One', he who is loves us more than anybody else. My existence did matter to him. Somebody was able to, and did care about all of my needs, all of my emotions, and stood before God and pleaded for me. Nobody on earth could fully provide for all of my needs, could always be there at every point, could respond continually to me. But there was someone in heaven who could and did. This person had my name graven on his hands and written on his heart. This person could not and did not forget me. My existence so mattered to him that he was willing to die to ensure that I lived. Through his death he could identify with the pain cancer caused me and was there in my loneliness. What's more, nothing could take this person away from me.

While Jesus allowed his brothers and sisters to care for me, he would not allow them to take his ultimate place. He taught me through the darker times to turn to him first and foremost, to take my hurt, pain and loneliness to him. He allowed the trial to show me my need of him and now I know where I must first turn to with everything.

Notes

1 Michael Skloff, Marta Kauffman, David Crane, Phil Solem, Allee Willis, Danny Wilde, I'll be there for you (© 1995 Til Dawn Music, CA, USA Warner/Chappell North America, London W6 8BS)
2 Everclear, *Wonderful*
3 Charitie L Bancroft (1841–92), *Before the Throne of God Above*

5. I Cannot Tell[1]

Shortly after starting chemotherapy I began preparation for radiotherapy. I had a few sessions where I lay on a table and people measured me, drew on me and even gave me tattoos, all in preparation for six weeks of daily treatment.

Radiotherapy is a weird treatment. Lasers are targeted directly at the tumour to kill off the cancer cells. It's a radioactive treatment which can do a lot of harm to your body. Yet you don't feel a thing as it takes place.

Of course it has side effects and you feel those. I was warned that the treatment could make me feel very tired. My skin could react as it would to sunburn. I was told to drink vast amounts of water and to use various moisturisers. The water drinking wasn't too difficult, although every time I had an alcoholic drink I was to drink double that amount of water. Two pints of water takes the fun out of a pint. Maybe that was the aim. As with the instructions I was given before chemotherapy there were warnings and much to fear. I understand why the thought of this treatment scares people but I didn't feel too scared. I don't know why. It wasn't bravery, more like immaturity. I decided not to think about it too much rather than facing the reality of the situation. It was all so new to me it was easy to pretend it wasn't real. While others would have wanted to know all the facts, how did the machine work, what were the statistics, what were the success rates, how many accidents happened etc etc, I preferred not to know. I didn't hit the Internet to see what I could find. I had to force myself to read the information pamphlets I was given. Learning that I would need to drink lots of water and apply cream was about as far as I wanted to go. I faced the treatment like a child, not really understanding what was going on but knowing I had to be a brave boy and go and do as I was told. I didn't underestimate the work of my amazing prayer army. I'm sure their prayers upheld me.

Radiotherapy for bowel cancer, as with many other cancers, was embarrassing. I soon had to get used to lying, trousers and undies down, while armies of people gave their full attention to my well moisturised rear end. Thankfully, I had my first preparation tests the day I was released from hospital, after my chemotherapy line had become infected. I was too tired to be bothered with embarrassment. It was an odd feeling, being moved into position. As they pushed and pulled me around I soon learnt that I wasn't being helpful by trying to move where they wanted me and had to fight the urge not to wriggle around. I had to lie in a position similar to when having a massage, face down, looking through a hole. I could never quite get my face comfortable squashed against the head rest. I remember hearing voices all around and it felt like the whole hospital was in the room. There was lots of measuring and drawing. They had to make sure they lined up the lasers pointing at exactly the right place. They only wanted the cancer targeted, nothing else, especially down there. As the lasers passed straight through my body it was important to get the angle right. Tiny tattoo dots were used to help line up the machines. I'm ticklish and with so many cold hands at work, it was difficult to keep still. Lots of scans were taken. It seemed to go on for ever but eventually it was over. I had the odd experience of having my trousers pulled up; not since childhood has that been done for me. Once I was decent they took my photo. I dread to think what I looked like.

You have a few preparation visits before the real thing. Once I got started, I soon got used to the routine. I went in, dropped the drawers, laid down, untangled the chemotherapy tubes which always seemed to wrap around me at that point and tried to get comfortable. The worst bit was lying there while they got me into position. I probably shouldn't say this but I did prefer it when the guy sorted me out, instead of the girls. Firstly, he had warm hands. I won't be publishing the findings of my survey but from the experiences of those weeks I found that men have warm hands, women have cold. Secondly, he had the physical strength to get me into the right position quickly. It always took the girls longer and involved a lot more uncomfortable pushing and pulling. After the initial measuring and lining up, they would all leave the room and the machine got to work. I couldn't see, having to lie face down and keep still, but the machine made strange clanking and buzzing noises around me. The gang would return for more measuring and the whole thing would be repeated a few more times.

It felt very lonely when they walked out of the room and the vast machine came to life. I realised that the lasers were pointing directly at me. Others may have understood how this machine worked, but it was pointed at me. I decided early on that dwelling on what was going on wasn't helpful and so I would use those times to pray. Holy, aren't I! I chose a different person each day and did my best to ignore the buzzing and humming. I also prayed for myself. It was a simple prayer. I prayed 'Make it work, make it work, make it work.' There didn't seem much point in more elaborate wording.

I had to go to Brighton for my treatment every day. I soon began to hate the A27 from Eastbourne. Despite the wonderful scenery it's not the nicest of roads in the rush hour. I think I must have been stationary on every inch of tarmac at some point during those six weeks. Most of my appointments seemed to be at times where I could not avoid the traffic. Getting there could take well over an hour. As with all hospital appointments, it was more likely that you would have to wait around than that things would follow the schedule. While I generally was only under the machines for around twenty to thirty minutes, the whole trip, door to door, usually took around three hours.

I'm very grateful to the radiographers. They were professional and made the whole experience quite bearable. They were also kind, making me feel that I was in safe, if at times cold, hands. The Macmillan nurses were great and certainly helped me through the whole process. The NHS receives so much criticism. I want to say that I was impressed again and again with the set-up of the cancer unit in Brighton and the chemotherapy ward in Eastbourne and very much appreciate the work of the people who treated and cared for me.

* * *

Missing half of each working day did not help my frustration levels. Throughout, I was able to drive myself to each appointment and to an extent organise my days around the treatment. Being on chemotherapy as well meant I had at least one afternoon visit to the chemotherapy ward in Eastbourne each week. Yet with the aid of a laptop I managed to stay involved in the final preparations for At Work Together. I mainly focused on how we were going to staff the event, who was going to do what and when. Delegation has always been one of my strong points so writing staff job descriptions and arranging work rotas came naturally. Considering my lack of conference experience, it was amazing that anybody took any notice of what I said. It did feel good to be of use in the final days.

Day one of the conference arrived. Early on the Sunday morning the team assembled in the lobby of the Devonshire Park Complex in Eastbourne. Only two of the group were not ill at that point, and if I say that I was one of the two then you'll understand the seriousness of the situation. Everyone seemed to have either a cold or a headache and most of them shouldn't have been working. We did wonder how on earth we would get things off the ground. All I can say is that Spring Harvest staff are made of strong stuff. I've often heard people say that it's amazing that Spring Harvest the main event ever happens, that order comes out of the chaos. Working on the inside I have been guilty of thinking the same thing. But it always does come together and a lot of this is down to the flexibility and sheer determination of the wonderful staff. With tissues in hand, to wipe noses not tears I might add, everyone set to work and by the time the first delegates arrived we had the main venue up and running and an impressive Arrivals and Information desk ready. The delegate registration was calm and professional, from the delegates' point of view at least! As they sat in the preliminary session on Day 2, everybody worked extremely hard to set up the remaining venues, the last one being finished as the delegates walked in to their first seminars. Of course I was nowhere to be seen, stuck over in Brighton doing nothing much, waiting to see a doctor. I returned to find some tired staff but everything was up and running and from that point on everything went to plan.

I didn't go to many of the teaching sessions but enjoyed hearing Rob Parsons speak on the first night. He said something I found really helpful. He said that the will of God was a broad path. I had often heard it taught that the will of God was a narrow path, that he knew the course of your life and there was only one route mapped out for you. You could choose to walk on that narrow path or sinfully choose your own way that would get you into trouble. I have seen people spend hours praying to find God's one and perfect will for them. This teaching did not sit comfortably with me or my experiences. I have come to the opinion that God gives us an incredible amount of freedom and allows us to make the majority of the choices which shape our life. I'm not saying that there aren't times he clearly says 'No, don't do it', to many things. There are things which we shouldn't do, paths we shouldn't take. However, I believe God says 'Yes' more than he says 'No'. He allows us to make choices about where we go, what we do and who we want to be. He has an incredible ability to let us choose yet to still bring about what he has planned for our lives. Rob Parsons was talking about the world of work and highlighting that there were many things a person could do for God in their workplace. However, for me, understanding that I was on a broad path with various options available to me helped me to understand how I tackled the issues of healing.

This is maybe a tenuous link but most Christians I've met believe that God is powerful enough to heal sickness. There is no illness that God cannot deal with, no power able to defeat God. I don't find it difficult to accept God's ultimate power as I believe he is the Creator of the universe. A God who was able to create my body is able to heal anything that is wrong with it. It seems to me that the question most Christians struggle with is not 'Can he?' but 'Will he?' Will God step into my life and get rid of my sickness so that I am 100% well and able to get on with my life? There are so many different beliefs surrounding whether God will heal or not but this is not an issue to be discussed purely in a theological way. It is an issue which strikes direct into the experiences and the hearts of anyone who is sick.

In the first few weeks following my diagnosis, I was unable to face the issue of healing. When people talked to me about God's healing power, I would be overcome with a wave of unpleasant emotions. It was difficult to put my finger exactly on how I felt but it involved feelings of fear, hurt, guilt and worry. Fear that God didn't care enough about me to bother to heal me. Hurt that I was having to go through illness in the first place. Guilt that I had done something to deserve my sickness. Worry that I wasn't doing something that I had to do to be healed. I could be happily getting along with my day, coping quite well, and the mention of being healed would instantly change my mood and lead me into despair. Thankfully I was protected from too many people giving their opinions about healing by my friends, who would stick close to me, stepping in and changing the direction of a conversation, or filtering messages when people had things they felt they should tell me.

To be blunt, when well-meaning people spoke to me about what they believed regarding God healing people, when they sent me books about God's promises to heal with examples of people who had claimed their healing, it hurt me deeply and caused me much confusion. Unless you know a person very well and have an open relationship with them, be very careful what you say to a sick person on this subject. It's not an easy issue, there are no easy answers and you can hurt people deeply at the point where they are most vulnerable.

I had heard it said that the Bible is full of promises that God wishes to and does heal. You have to believe these promises and have faith that he can heal and then you can be healed. I struggled with this teaching, fundamentally because I believed it on so many levels. Throughout the Bible I read verse after verse where God promised good health to those who trusted in him. Faith seemed to play a role in the gospel accounts of healings; 'Go, your faith has made you well.' I believed that you can take hold of verses and claim them for yourself. But, and it was a big one, I had seen people do it and die. I knew of people, good people with amazing faith, who had contracted serious illnesses. Their churches had been motivated to pray like never before and people had taken hold of verse after verse but the person died. I had to conclude that while God promised to heal, he didn't always seem to do it in every case.

One of the reasons I found it so hard to talk about God healing me was that I felt I didn't have enough faith to claim my healing, to believe it into reality. It made me feel like a failure. If my healing depended on my level of faith, I was well and truly stuffed. I didn't really understand what faith meant. On one hand I felt I had plenty of faith. Since God had shown up in my life in the first week of having cancer I had not doubted his existence. I had no problem believing God was real, all powerful, my Creator, well able to heal me. I knew he listened to my prayers, and could see him answering many of them. Yet my faith still didn't seem to be of the mustard seed sized proportions needed to move a pebble, let alone a mountain. I liked mountains, much nicer than a flat plain, and had never felt inclined to throw one in the sea. My car, on the other hand, was far more moveable than a mountain; it rolled on wheels for a start. When it broke down I was more than inclined to move it but my faith had never budged it an inch, even with the handbrake off! I hadn't ever had any success in claiming a healing over a cold, so cancer felt completely out of my league. I had so many questions, not many answers, and in many ways it was all too much for me to face at that point.

A favourite hymn brought me comfort at this point, *I Cannot Tell*. This hymn reminded me that there were many others Christians who didn't know all the answers. Each verse began with a list of things which the author 'couldn't tell', yet midway through each verse the direction swung on the word 'but'; 'But this I know'. Following a list of things the hymn writer didn't know, came a list of those he did know. The verses finished on the positive. I like the word 'but'. It seemed to give validity to our doubts and questions yet does not allow them to have the final word. It allows the negative but leads to the positive.

I didn't know why God appeared to heal sometimes and other times not, but I knew that God brought salvation to those who had a mustard seed of faith, just enough to turn to him and say 'Help!' He had answered the cry of those who weren't even sure he was there listening to them at all. I knew that if Jesus' death on the cross guaranteed me both healing and eternal life then, just as I needed only a tiny seed of faith to claim the promise of eternal life, the same was needed to claim healing. I wondered that in the same way as we would all die on this earth before we entered eternal life in heaven, we might have to die of our illnesses before we were fully healed in eternity.

Eventually, having had to work through various thoughts in my head, I came to a realisation that changed how I felt about the whole subject of healing. I didn't know if I was going to die of cancer but I knew that I wasn't going to have cancer in heaven. As much as my eternal life was guaranteed, so was my eternal life without cancer.

I know that some people reading this will shake their heads because to them I will have missed the point. They will be able to put together an argument that the Bible teaches I can be healed now and that illness should have no place in a Christian's life. I wish I could accept it but the question will always haunt me, why then do some die? Books have been written about this, and those I've looked at don't provide me with an answer. In fact, they often sicken me when they give reasons why people are not healed. Also, I've never seen any mention of why those who are healed eventually die, although maybe I'm being childish here. But this I know, no illness is the end, no sickness is defeat, even if we die. My mustard seed of faith is big enough for me to claim, I will be healed.

Why didn't God heal me as soon as I was diagnosed with cancer? I believe he wanted me to see a bigger picture, to catch a glimpse of my own eternal nature, to show me a little of how he regards sickness. At that point, as radiotherapy began, as I struggled to understand what God had to say about healing, I realised that there was not a narrow path ahead of me. It was not a case that I had to believe certain things, do specific things and I would be healed. It was not the case that if I made a mistake, didn't believe the right things with the correct level of faith, that I would fall off the narrow path and die of cancer. God's path was broad. He would allow me to walk along with my doubts, my fears. He would allow me to make choices but as I trusted him he would take me to where he wanted me to go.

The biggest choice I had to make was would I take the treatment offered to me, would I have chemotherapy and radiotherapy? I could have chosen to say 'No', that I would trust God to answer my prayers and heal me. I chose treatment but not out of a lack of faith. I believed God had given humanity much wisdom and that doctors had been given the knowledge to heal. I believed that God healed in many ways, the broad path again. Sometimes he would step in directly and heal in an instant, other times he would wait. Sometimes it would involve treatment and other times it wouldn't. Either way, what he ordained would come to pass. To me this wasn't fatalistic but a step of faith, faith that God controlled my destiny, did have a plan, a faith step that said that I would believe in a God able to weave out of the choices I made the life he wished me to live. I chose treatment and God used the experiences in the moulding process of making the new me.

There was a line in the Mel Gibson film *The Passion* that has helped me further understand how God's way of working isn't always what we expect. Amidst what to others looks like chaos and defeat, God can be at work. The greatest example of this is the death of Jesus. As everybody looked on, he was mercilessly beaten, made to carry his cross, and ultimately killed in the most painful of ways. It seemed that Jesus was defeated. If Jesus was the Messiah then it looked as if even God had been defeated. Yet millions of people have known that this was all part of God's mysterious plan. The film was horrific, yet from the moment at the beginning of the film where Jesus crushed the snake's head under foot, I felt I was watching something victorious. Shortly before I watched the film, I went to see *Jesus Christ Superstar*. This musical seemed to portray Jesus as a victim, unable to understand who he was and unable to stop his death. In contrast, I noticed many clues in Gibson's film that while the events tortured Jesus, he knew who he was and knew what he was doing.

The line that spoke to me and brought tears to my eyes was spoken by Jesus to Mary as he carried his cross through the streets of Jerusalem to Calvary. That journey seemed to take for ever. How could he carry his cross on his beaten back, let alone bear the hateful taunts? If I'm honest, I wanted him just to give in and die there on the road. It seemed too much for one man to carry on going at all, let alone fight so much to get to a place of even greater torture. Death there on the road seemed a kindness. Mary was pushing her way through the crowd to reach him but couldn't get through. She was taken down a side passage and turned back onto the main route just as Jesus passed. He stumbled and she ran to him. He turned and said to Mary, 'See, I make all things new.' That line struck so deep a chord within me and showed me the true victory of what Jesus did. Out of suffering he made something new. I wanted to stand in the cinema and shout, 'That is the Jesus I believe in.' I realised that God's ways are not our ways and how he works is so different from what we expect. The crowd, looking on, thought Jesus was on his final way to destruction, but in reality he was in the process of making everything new. Out of hurt, pain and suffering came life.

No matter how many sermons I hear explaining why Jesus had to die, had to be a sacrifice, had to atone for my sin, I still have a part of my brain that says 'I don't get it ... why?' Wiser people may understand but still I wonder if there could have been another way. I just have to accept God works in ways I do not always understand, and yet he is able, out of suffering, to make things new.

I am not for one moment linking what I went through to the horrific suffering of Christ, but I realised as I heard Jesus say that line, 'See, I make all things new', that through the difficulties I had worked through, the hurt, the pain associated with my treatment, he had indeed been with me and had been making me new. God's way of working in me confused me in a similar way to how his way of working through Jesus' suffering and death confused me. But my heart leapt as I heard that line and in an instant realised that I was one of the things he was making new.

What I want to convey to the person facing illness and all the difficulty it brings is this, don't feel there is only one way forward and if you get it wrong, you are doomed. Don't feel you have to have all the answers. Don't feel you can only earn your healing through your own faith. God longs for your salvation and your healing more than you do. There is a point to what you go through, and there is a reason why God acts as he acts. Hold on to what you do know, seek God with all your heart. That's what he wants more than anything else, for you to seek him, regardless of circumstances.

I may have lost a reader or two along the way here, disgusted that I am unable to offer clear-cut teaching. I didn't set out to write a book of answers and I'm not a theologian. I was, and still am, a traveller on a journey of faith and have written about what I experienced, felt and learnt. To those who believe Christianity is a set of answers to logical questions I must look like a ship lost at sea. But I believe that there is room for mystery in Christianity, room for the unanswered question coupled with a need to hold on by faith to what we do know. God is able to cope with my questions, even the difficult ones surrounding why people die from sickness. I needed to learn to accept that God does not always answer in the way I may want.

When discussing the mystery of how God sometimes acts I was directed to this quote by Dennis Covington, in turn quoted by Philip Yancey in his book *Reaching for the Invisible God*: 'Mystery is not the absence of meaning, but the presence of more meaning than we can comprehend.'[2]

One day I'll know the answers. Until then I need to be the faithful servant, believing that God can and does heal, but more importantly, believing that he knows what he's doing.

Notes

1 William Young Fullerton (1857–1932), *I Cannot Tell*
2 Dennis Covington, *Salvation on Sand Mountain* (New York: Penguin, 1995), p204

6. Are You Lord God Almighty?[1]

Do you ever feel that it's the little things shoved onto the top of the pile that cause you to drop everything, not the big things? Despite being attached to my chemotherapy pump, despite daily radiotherapy appointments, it was a little infection that turned up at the wrong moment which ruined all my careful planning. I had wanted more than anything to go to as much of the At Work Together conference as possible. I was extremely pleased when the first day arrived and I was able to go. No sudden hospital stays, no sickness, no mad gun-waving neighbours, all was well. My car wouldn't start on the Sunday morning but I had not let that get in the way, quickly dumping it and finding transport from other places. I began that Sunday feeling fine, on top of the world. By the end of the day I was beginning to feel rough.

There's no polite way of telling the story without being direct. Exactly one year previously I had had a boil. I can remember the exact date, as it was just before I went to the Evangelical Alliance Assembly in Cardiff. People may snigger and not take boils seriously, until they have one. They are horrible. Not only are they uncomfortable but they make you feel washed out and sick. Antibiotics cleared it up the first time round. I couldn't believe it when, after all that had happened, it chose the first day of the conference to return. I tried to ignore it until the Monday morning when I mentioned it to the radiographers during my treatment. They sent me to see the duty doctor. I had to spend the morning waiting to be seen. Understanding my desire to spend as little time at the hospital on the three days of the conference, I had kindly been given the first radiotherapy appointment for the three days of the conference. If all had gone to plan, I would have been back in Eastbourne by 10am. Instead, I found myself waiting for over an hour, only to be examined and told that they would leave it a day to see what happened. I returned to the conference to find everything running smoothly. As the day went on I felt more and more ill and uncomfortable. I was staying in a hotel in Eastbourne and was very ready for my bed that night. However, I was feeling too rough to sleep.

By two o'clock in the morning I was beside myself. I was so angry that this stupid infection had come back at the time when I could do without it. A week later and I could have coped. Forget having cancer, I was more wound up by it than anything else I had to put up with during treatment. I totally lost it that night. I wanted to smash something, wanted to take my frustration out on someone or something. Thankfully I realised that smashing something in a hotel room paid for by my employers wouldn't be a good idea. I stuffed a pillow into my mouth and screamed as loud as I could. It was something I've never done before or since. The only way I could deal with the anger and frustration was to scream. Maybe it was lucky I was in a hotel room and had to cover the noise, or maybe it would have been better to have been elsewhere and just let it all out. All I know is that I could no longer hold in the feelings, no longer put on a brave face and it was easier to throw a tantrum.

Why tell this bit? It's a warts, boils and all story. At each step along the journey there were times when I felt amazingly strong in God, able to cope with what was going on around me, able to hold my life together. I wasn't putting on a brave face; when I was happy I was actually happy. My faith didn't mean that life went from strength to strength, though. There were setbacks, times of despair, times when I didn't say prayers, read Scriptures or shout hallelujah, but screamed into my pillow. I would keep this part of the tale to myself if I didn't think that there are others out there who scream into their pillows. Sometimes it's all you can do at that point. Just don't fall into the trap of thinking you are the only person who does it.

I had to be driven to radiotherapy the next day, unable to manage myself. I saw my specialist by chance while waiting for my radiotherapy appointment. By now I was looking pale and the smart suit couldn't hide that something was wrong. She referred me to a surgeon in Eastbourne who agreed to see me that afternoon. My 'in and out no fuss' plan fell to pieces and I knew that I would lose most of the day to the dreaded hospital waiting room. It was the strangest of days. Dressed in my finest suit (my only suit, actually) I sat in waiting rooms. I had a few hours break between the Brighton bit and the Eastbourne bit so went back to the conference and chatted to a few speakers and a few delegates. I checked various staff members were happy then, before I knew it, the suit was hanging up and I was in a gown, lying on a trolley and waiting for a quick bit of on the spot surgery. An hour later I was back in the suit, hobnobbing once again.

I am a planner. I like to look ahead and decide what I will do, where and when. I had had some success in planning my days to fit in chemotherapy, radiotherapy, a conference for five hundred delegates, blood tests, fertility treatment, staff training sessions, scans and endless appointments. A little boil upset my careful timetabling. My frustration was fuelled by more than daily interruptions to my diary. I feared that this disease was going to affect my long-term plans to have a career, my own family, and to watch events unfold in the lives of my friends and relatives. I found I had to hold my plans lightly, not making them so important that I couldn't cope if things didn't go as I intended. Ultimately, I had to trust my hopes and dreams, my plans and aspirations to God and learn to trust that he was in control. I found this incredibly hard.

It has been my experience that God hasn't asked me to give up my organising nature. I believe he has given me gifts which he has been able to use. However, through having cancer, I learnt that if we say we are followers of God then we do have to make our plans secondary to those he has for us. Working through these challenges showed me some positive aspects of my character that it did me good to identify. I learnt that I could walk out of an operation, admittedly a minor one, put on a suit and go and do my job. I learnt that I could face despair and still get up and get on. I learnt that I was someone with the internal strength not to let cancer ruin my life. I'm not telling you this to boast, please believe me. I'm sharing this to encourage others facing difficult times and feeling they are failures. I have learnt that I judge myself too harshly and drive myself far too hard. I don't think I'm alone. Christians in particular are prone to doing this. I'm always hearing people say they are no good, poor at having their quiet time with God, slow to help others, of little use in the church. Often these people appear to me to have hearts of gold, to serve God with so much energy, and always be putting others first.

Maybe we need to stop now and then and see what we are getting right, what has gone well, what we are good at. I needed to. If you are going through hard times, if all seems hopeless and you are finding yourself hating who you are, be brave. Stop, have a close look at yourself. You may see strengths and beauty in your character which are influencing how you are responding to the situation. Maybe you will begin, with time, to see how God is using the circumstances to bring positive changes in your life.

* * *

Holy Holy
Are You Lord God Almighty
Worthy is the Lamb
Worthy is the Lamb
You are Holy.[2]

Why this song for this chapter? This is a powerful song which sounds awesome when sung by four thousand in a Spring Harvest Big Top. When I sing the line 'Are You Lord God Almighty' my heart is asking the question, 'Are you? Are you holy? Are you almighty?' I can't help asking even when worshipping. How I don't get hit by a thunderbolt, I do not know. I have discovered that God is strong enough to cope with this question. If you choose, in the face of hardship, to trust God, to give your life to him, I believe it's a valid question to ask. In so many ways he answers it.

The conference finished well. Stabbing a boil does wonders and I was fine on the final day. I had one of those lovely moments that make any amount of effort worthwhile. I met a delegate whom I had spoken to a few months earlier. He had wanted to cancel his booking and asked for a refund. I'm not the greatest at marketing but as I spoke to this guy, I felt the conference would be of value to him. He was a businessman whose work life took up a lot of his time and energy. He felt his church didn't value or support him in what he did. Instead he felt judged for not devoting more time to church life. He was trying to balance the demands of work, home and church. The conference focused on work/life balance. I felt this guy would benefit so much from the teaching. We bumped into each other on the last evening. He had met God, felt loved and valued. He had learnt so much that would help him in his life. He was full of thanks for the conference. God whispered in my ear, 'See, I am Almighty.'

Notes

1 Michael W Smith, *Agnus Dei* (© 1990 Milene Music Incorporated, USA. Acuff Rose Music Ltd. All rights reserved. International copyright secured)

2 Michael W Smith, *Agnus Dei* (© 1990 Milene Music Incorporated, USA. Acuff Rose Music Ltd. All rights reserved. International copyright secured)

7. No One's Life is More Real than Yours[1]

I finished the conference on a high. I had new vision and ideas about what I could do next. I forgot cancer for a few moments, focused ahead, wanting a new challenge. I had to be a good boy and do what everyone wanted me to do, to cut back on the work and take it easy for a bit. I did plan to rest but it took a few days to calm down. As the adrenalin wore off I began to feel the effects of the weeks of chemotherapy and radiotherapy. I became increasingly tired. Simple tasks sapped all my strength. I found that if I overdid it I paid for it by feeling rough. My skin was reacting to the lasers and I began to find it difficult to sit down comfortably. It could have been a lot worse. I got off lightly but I had to make adjustments to cope with the treatment.

I didn't like having to set aside my desire to find a new work challenge and my eagerness to plan ahead. But I didn't have a choice. My body was refusing to keep up. The nurses in the chemotherapy ward grassed me up to my oncologist for rushing to appointments and falling asleep in the day room. I was kindly reproved and told to take life at a much slower pace. I didn't find it easy to comply despite everyone ganging up on me. I've already said, I'm no workaholic, I love my free time. I can happily spend the whole day lazing on my sofa lost in a book or watching a film. You would have thought I would enjoy being told to sit back and do nothing. Before this happened I would have thought I would enjoy the free time, but there's something different about time off when you are feeling rough. I didn't find I could concentrate for long on a book or a film. I wanted to get outside and go for a good long walk but didn't have the energy. I could sleep for hours but wake up not feeling refreshed. It was hard to remain positive. I continued to drive myself to Brighton each day and that helped break up the days but there was something so dispiriting when I looked back on the day and realised that I had not accomplished much at all.

I'm a daydreamer and found it easy to create fantasy worlds in my head, worlds where I wasn't ill. I enjoy the holiday programmes and dreamed of being a researcher, going ahead of the film crew, trying out the activities, visiting the sites, enjoying the culture. I also imagined an ordinary life with a nine to five office job, a life where little happened but I was content and cancer had no part. I had a dog to take for walks and a few hobbies for the weekend. The problem with these daydreams was that I began to want to be somebody else, not to be me. Everyone else's life looked better, and of course a life without cancer, free from the struggles of daily treatment and the fears of the future, was most likely a tad more fun. The hard reality was that I couldn't be somebody else.

I don't think it's too negative to look at those worse off than you to bring a bit of perspective. This was easily done visiting the cancer wards each day. I saw so many people in much worse situations than I was; people without hair, with pale skin, in obvious discomfort. In contrast I hadn't lost my hair. In fact the chemotherapy gave me a slightly tanned look and some people asked if I had been on a winter holiday! My discomfort wasn't stopping me driving, getting around and living a fairly normal life. Only once in all those waiting rooms did I see someone younger than me. She had lost all her hair. There is something about a lady losing her hair that seems so tragic. I couldn't help but feel sorry for her.

There is a danger in looking at others and considering yourself to be in a far worse condition, for you don't really know what is going on inside their skin. I was the victim of this one time in the waiting room. I was having a rough day and my skin was sore. I was referred to the resident doctor by the radiographer. I had to go and wait in the main waiting room where all the drivers and family wait. It was a busy day, made worse by heavy rain which always creates such a horrible atmosphere in crowded waiting rooms. I had to stand for a bit and was so relieved when a seat became available. I was worried I might collapse.

More people came in. Everyone was much older than I by far and I began to notice cross faces looking in my direction. As the youngest there people obviously thought I should give up my seat. I was sure people were muttering about the rude young man. I had to go to the radiotherapy waiting room and ask if I could sit there to escape the glares. I'm not after sympathy, although any given will be gratefully received. The point is that those around me judged wrongly. I wasn't a young driver waiting to pick up a elderly relative. I wasn't the prime candidate for giving up my chair. I could barely stand up!

Despite the positives and negatives of comparing your situation with those around you, it's hard not to dream of a different life. My life was no longer the life that I wanted to live. I felt I was living in the second best. Surely the best life that I could live would be one in which I was healthy and strong, a life where I could build on the enthusiasm that the conference had created within me, a life of success.

Christians face another danger at this point. They can begin to believe that they have missed God's best for their lives. They can begin to ask if they have done something wrong which has shunted them off the spiritual highway onto the dirt track. In one sense the answer is, at times, yes. Christian or non, being a chain smoker leads many to have lung cancer. The teenage couple who sleep together can't really claim they are blameless when the baby arrives. The course of their lives will be permanently changed. However, many of the things which come our way and alter our course are not the consequences of our actions and when things go wrong it is easy to become bitter. Some get angry with God, some get angry with themselves. Either way, there is disappointment that life hasn't gone the way they had hoped.

I fell into the trap of wishing I could be someone else, for surely anybody's life was better than mine. I couldn't believe that this was the life that God would want me to live. At that point I wasn't angry with God, but I was disappointed with him. My brother gave me a book which really helped me; *Second Choice: Embracing life as it is* by Viv Thomas.[2] The book used the biblical character Daniel as an example of someone whose life didn't follow the path that he would have wanted. When Daniel was considering his future as a young boy I doubt he would have chosen to be taken in exile to a land far from his home. Despite his many achievements and adventures in Babylon, I bet Daniel's first choice would have been to remain in his homeland. Yet, look how God was able to use Daniel.

Viv Thomas uses the term 'second choice worlds' to describe the life many have to live which isn't the one they would plan for themselves, not their first choice world. Daniel's second choice world was Babylon and the life of an exile. Having cancer pushed me into my second choice world. My first choice life would not involve me having cancer. I would be successful in what I did, happy with my job. I'd be well off, comfortable and do exciting things. I would want to be a valuable member of my church and to see good spiritual growth in my life. The reality was different. At a young age I had a life-threatening illness which involved having dangerous treatment which I couldn't ignore; it affected me every day.

Viv Thomas suggests that second choice worlds are not second best worlds. They are the worlds that God intended us to live in and there are lessons to be learnt, through the experiences thrust upon us. Daniel embraced his second choice world. He saw success and God was able to use him mightily. In fact, throughout the Bible we see that God uses trials and difficulties as his tools. They are not always the result of his displeasure with us, in fact they are often the opposite. They are a sign that he cares enough to want to mould our lives into something amazing. The pressures of our second choice worlds bring out hidden depths in our characters. They can help us find who we really are. We can be pushed to learn new things and to find skills we didn't know we had. It's not an easy way to grow and learn, but don't fall for the trap of believing there is no value to the suffering.

There is a value to what we go through, a lesson to be learnt, a gem to find. I love this quote from Henri J. M. Nouwen's *With Burning Hearts* that Viv Thomas uses to start his chapter three:

Somehow, in the midst of our tears, a gift is hidden.
Somehow, in the midst of our mourning, the first steps of the dance take place.
Somehow, the cries that well up from our losses belong to our song of gratitude.

This book helped me embrace my situation. I stopped wishing to be someone else, wanting another life. I began to search for the 'Treasures in the hidden place'. I began to hope that my situation was going to be of value. I set some new goals, one of which I hope is coming to pass as I write this book, for my story to be of help to someone else.

A good friend of mine wrote the song from which this chapter gets its title. In the song, sports stars and pop stars are shown as examples of people who we may wish to be, people who we think are better than us, people who live more real lives than we do. As Christians we can fall for the trap of looking at others who seem to be much better people, better Christians than us. We can start to believe that others have wonderful lives without anything going wrong. More dangerously, we can think that we must be worse people for going through difficult times, we must have done something wrong. Maybe you did do something which has a consequence you have to live with. But also consider that God could be trying to teach you something.

The Bible is full of heroes but look closely, they all had hardships to face. I don't believe there is a super spiritual highway inhabited by people who never face hardship, who always get to live in their first choice worlds. We all have our own journey and no one's life is better than the one God gave each one of us.

* * *

Even though I walk through the valley of the shadow of death ... Psalm 23:4

One of the treasures I found was that God was with me in the dark times. It's a precious jewel to find, to know that God is there no matter what is going on around you.

As I came near the end of my radiotherapy and into the final month of my chemotherapy I began to focus on the end of my treatment. I naively thought I was nearly there. When I was first diagnosed I was warned that a possible six months of treatment lay ahead. Surgery could then have followed. I'm not sure where I got the impression that surgery was unlikely, or that my first twelve weeks of chemotherapy would probably be all that would be needed. The first consultations were a bit of a blur. However, I did check with the various people who had sat with me and we were all in agreement. We had all understood that I would have twelve weeks of chemotherapy, six of radiotherapy and that surgery was not necessarily on the cards. I was looking forward to it all being over.

I have learnt when dealing with cancer that the doctors do not have many definite answers. They can't say 'If you do this this and this the result will be...' Different tumours react in different ways to treatment. The pace of research into different chemotherapy drugs means that new drugs come quickly onto the market but the full results, however successful they are, can't be seen until five or so years later. Five years seems to be the magic number. If you get to five years and the cancer has not returned, you are judged to be in the clear, more or less. I suppose I believed that doctors know what to do to make you well. It's a lot more complicated than that.

I had been told from the start that it was unusual for someone my age to have bowel cancer. I was also told that the way the cancer had spread into the lymph gland was unusual. My cancer wasn't acting in the way that bowel cancers generally acted. While it was described as aggressive cancer I'm not sure anyone really knew how it would react to the treatment. Somewhere along the line the team who discussed my case and considered what was the best treatment had decided that I would probably need surgery. The aim of the radiotherapy and chemotherapy would be to reduce the tumour to a size which could be removed. They no longer expected the radiotherapy and chemotherapy to be enough. Unfortunately, no one noticed that I hadn't been told.

I found out by accident. In the last week of my radiotherapy I was put on a different machine which targeted the area in the groin where I had the lump removed. I had been given different schedules. One showed that I would be having this new treatment in addition to the normal daily radiotherapy treatment, the other showed the new treatment would replace the old. I was having the trial run for the new machine with all the measuring and drawing. I asked my oncologist why the treatment seemed to be changing from the first plan. She said that they had done enough radiotherapy on the tumour and that they were preparing me for surgery.

I thought that people were exaggerating when they said that their heart missed a beat when told some difficult news. I now get what they mean. There was a pause, my brain pondered whether I'd heard correctly, I had, and a wave of panic washed over me. The nurse in the room must have noticed the change in me and suggested that we talk after the session. I was sent off for my normal radiotherapy treatment. I lay there going over it all in my head again and again. She can't mean what I think she means. I must have misunderstood. I don't think I have ever fought so hard to control myself; I was battling against a fear that kept threatening to take over.

I was shown into a little consultation room. My oncologist came and spoke to me. She did mean that they were considering surgery, which would result in me having a permanent colostomy bag. They would remove a large section of the bowel to get rid of as much of the affected area as possible. This would give me the greatest chance of keeping the cancer at bay. That's about all I can remember of that conversation. I lost the control I was fighting so hard to keep and began to cry. I don't think she knew what to do with me and she left to find the Macmillan nurse. He wasn't available so one of the radiographers came with tissues and a cup of tea. I couldn't bring myself under control. I got through most of the tissue box. I was left alone and nobody came back. I was in such a state I didn't feel I could walk out of the room, across the crowded waiting room, to find out what was going on.

After half an hour I decided to go home. I had had enough of doctors and hospitals, enough of being told one thing and then something different happening. I was fed up with being confused. I was going home. Goodness knows what I looked like to the many people I had to pass to get out of there and across the street to my car. I got on my mobile and phoned a friend. I could barely speak, I was in shock. I phoned my parents who set off from London immediately. Everyone was concerned about me driving home in that state but I couldn't bear asking anyone to battle through the rush hour traffic to come and get me. It was dark, raining, busy and a horrid drive home.

Mark came and stayed with me until my parents arrived. I don't think I've ever been more grateful for them turning up to look after me. I didn't care about being independent at that point. I didn't want to be a grown up, I wanted to be a boy and be looked after. I was so grateful to have them there to fight my battles.

We went back to the hospital the next day. We were angry and wanted answers. I feel sorry for the Macmillan guy as it wasn't really anything to do with him but he bore the brunt of our frustrations. Yesterday's mug and tissues were still in the room and I wondered if anybody had come to check that I wasn't still there before they locked up the night before. We couldn't see my oncologist, so appointments were made for the next week.

When we did get to see her we were given the facts. It wasn't clear if the chemotherapy and radiotherapy could reduce the tumour enough so that they could operate, but if it could, then an operation would be the next step. A decision was not going to be made instantly and I was told that I might have to have more chemotherapy. What appeared clear was that I wasn't coming to the end of my treatment, as I had thought.

In my nicer moments I'm more generous towards to the healthcare professionals. They deal with many people and mistakes can be made. With so many people caring for me it could easily be overlooked that facts hadn't been passed on. I also realise that they didn't give me all the facts at once, didn't hit me with cancer and colostomy bags in one go in case it was too much. It was unfortunate that the information was not given to me in a way I understood.

In other moods I can be quite cross with how things work. So often I felt that I wasn't given the whole picture of what was going on. I was also often given conflicting information about what was to happen and when. For example, I'd be told I'd have a certain scan at a certain time and it wouldn't happen. Exact answers were not given to questions. While I know it isn't always possible for doctors to say exactly what will happen, and there is a lot of 'wait and see' involved, I still think I could have been kept better informed. I'm the kind of person that would rather be told all the facts, no matter how hard, than to live with questions and doubts in my mind. The result of showing our displeasure at the NHS's handling of this little episode was that we agreed with my oncologist that I should be told everything that was going on. My concerns over the consequences of the surgery were noted. We were not at the point where any decisions had to be made. We agreed to put aside talk of an operation until after I'd finished radiotherapy and chemotherapy and they had a clearer picture of what would happen next.

I'm not innocent in all of this. I chose not to research too deeply into what bowel cancer was about and how it was treated. I chose ignorance rather than facing the reality of the situation. If I had looked at some of the literature given to me I would have realised that most people who have bowel cancer do have surgery. I chose to push any thoughts of operations and colostomy bags to the back of my mind and in doing so maybe set myself up for a shock. Perhaps I should have asked more questions all along, perhaps I was too laid back. I often felt stupid when others seemed to know more about what could happen. I also struggled to tell people what the doctors had said to me. After consultations people would want answers. What condition was the tumour in? Was the treatment working? What was going to happen next? I found myself caught between doctors who weren't giving me clear answers and friends and family who wanted things outlined in black and white. I was always kicking myself for not asking the doctors the most obvious questions, those that seemed completely obvious when someone asked them afterwards. It made me feel useless, not asking the right questions and not being able to answer the questions asked of me later. Sometimes I wouldn't tell people I had appointments at all so that I didn't have to do any reporting back. I gave myself a hard time.

I'm not so hard on myself now. I realise that the doctors often couldn't give straight answers because they just didn't know. I shouldn't have held myself responsible for not being able to answers questions. If I couldn't get straight answers, others couldn't expect them of me. That's hindsight for you! A word of warning, be gentle when asking your questions of an ill person.

* * *

… I will fear no evil, for you are with me.
Psalm 23:4

I saw a stoma nurse, I read the leaflets, I began to understand what it meant to have a stoma and a colostomy bag. I had heard of them but never realised what was involved. The more I found out, the less I wanted it. I accepted that people could live fairly normal active lives with the things but didn't want to have to try. I didn't want to look different, didn't want to have to think of appliances.

I could understand why the partner of someone having to have the surgery would stick by them afterwards and cope with the alteration of their loved one's body. The love they had before would hold them together. But I couldn't see how someone entering a relationship and finding their partner had a colostomy bag could overcome their repulsion at the thing and be physically attracted to them. I've learnt a bit more about love and relationships now and see things a bit differently but at that point I could only see the obstacles this thing would place in my way. I could only see myself as partially disabled, struggling to do the most simple things, single and unlovable. I grieved my first choice world.

I never got to the stage where a firm decision was made to proceed with surgery and so never had actually to prepare myself. I knew I would go through with it if I had to but I did question if my life would still be worth living. Was there enough to bring me satisfaction, happiness, enough to cover the difficulties that life with a colostomy would pose? The answer to this difficult question was 'Yes'. If I had a particularly good day with my friends I'd say to myself 'See, it would be worth sticking around for another day like that.' While driving, if I came across a particularly beautiful Sussex view I'd think about wanting to see it again. Even if I couldn't walk in this countryside I'd always be able to drive to places to look at it. At that time, seeing people in wheelchairs getting on with their lives brought a lot of perspective. I realised that life with a colostomy bag was nothing compared with what others had to face and yet they were getting on with their lives and enjoying them. The three guys dancing in their wheelchairs in the BBC clips in between pro-grammes showed me the life and energy within people far worse off than me. I tried to embrace my second choice world, accepting it despite it not being what I wanted.

Yet I felt surrounded by enemies; not people but thoughts and feelings. I would fall to sleep quickly at around 10pm but wake around 2am and be unable to get back to sleep. These were my toughest, darkest times. God felt a million miles away. I pleaded with him to come and help me sleep, to take away the fears that surrounded me and threatened to defeat me. I didn't want to break down. I didn't really know what it meant to have a breakdown. I wondered if I would just not get up in the morning, not care, not notice. I'd wake up able to get on with the day but then wonder why as night came I'd sink into a depressive state, fearing I was losing my mind.

I didn't understand why I was feeling like this. This cancer lark had been going on for four months. I had a new closeness to God since being diagnosed. I'd seen him help me, I'd seen him at work around me. Why now was I struggling so much? I thought I had no right to feel as I did, no right to be depressed. Yes, things were tough but God had shown he was with me. He'd provided so much support. By this point thousands of people were praying for me! Where was the victory promised to the Christian who stands on God's word? Why were the promises of his peace, his love, his healing not leading me out of this valley of death? Where was the treasure in the darkness?

I wondered if I was mildly schizophrenic. These dark times came at night but so often during the day I felt strong. During the day I felt God with me, I saw what he was teaching me, could see the value of the experiences. At night it left me completely. I saw no good around me at all. As time went on I felt I was losing the ability to be positive, upbeat, someone who could face the challenges before him. I couldn't understand why I was going down hill. I confided again in Andy while sitting in a pub having lunch. He told me I was grieving. I didn't realise this was what was going on. It had not entered my head before that point that I was in grief. I acquainted grief with the response to someone's death. It was a process, at times a necessary and healthy process, of mourning the loss of a loved one. I didn't think you could grieve the loss of your own life; not the physical reality of your own death, but the death of your hopes and dreams, the death of your first choice world.

You would not expect a person grieving for a lost loved one always to be positive, always to focus on the good things about the lost person's life and never be overcome with the pain of losing them. I realised that it was okay to grieve for myself, the loss of me. It was okay to grieve that I might die young, not have a wife, a family, a future. I learnt that living in Christian victory did not mean that I ignored the pain of my present circumstances. God did not expect me to pretend that the circumstances were not hurting me. He didn't need me to shout 'Praise the Lord, I'm having a colostomy.' He didn't need me, at that point, to put my reality into an eternal perspective. Of course in the light of the glories of heaven and the eternal life promised me the reality of my situation pales, not into insignificance, but it's not such a big deal. God did not need me to focus on this eternal perspective at that point. For some reason we grieve, and it's okay.

I looked through the gospels for the times where it said Jesus grieved. I was struck by Jesus' cry of pain when God turned away from him on the cross, unable to look upon the sin Jesus bore for us. Jesus knew what he was doing yet still at that point he grieved the temporary loss of his Father. Andy suggested that if I found God at my darkest point then I had truly found a great prize. When all is fine and dandy it is so much easier to believe in God's reality. If you find him in the darkness then you find a whole new dimension to his reality.

Strangely, coming to an understanding about my own grieving process stopped the sleepless nights. The understanding of the treasures I have found has been more rational and a bit less poetic. God didn't suddenly appear at 3am while I tossed and turned in my bed and say, *'Voilà* you've found me.' But the things I have learnt have been gems to hold on to. I learnt that as I walk through the dark valleys on my journey there is never a time when he is not there. It may feel like he isn't and I still don't completely know why that is, but he is there. He surrounds us, he protects us, and he won't let our enemies finish us off. My testimony now is that he has led me through and out of my dark valley of cancer. I imagine further dark valleys lie ahead, but he is and will be with me.

Karl Marx called religion the opiate of the people. There are different layers of meaning behind this quote. Certainly there seems to have been times when religion has been used to drug the people into inactivity and acceptance of some unjust circumstances. If you take this quote simply to mean that religion numbs the pain of real life then I suggest you try it. You'll soon find there is too much talc mixed with the opium, it doesn't numb the pain enough! But does religion help you through difficult times? My faith does.

Notes

1 Julian Shortman, *No One's Life is More Real Than Yours*
2 Viv Thomas, *Second choice: embracing life as it is,* (Carlisle: Paternoster, 2000)

8. I am His and He is Mine[1]

In Christ Alone is my favourite hymn. I like many hymns, old and new. I like the solid robust feel many have. They help me to focus my beliefs, to stand my ground and say with conviction, this is what I believe. I love the sound of a large congregation singing in unity. I'm a traditionalist when it comes to hymns. I love the tradition wrapped around the words, the fact that for many years Christians have sung these words and meant them. I also love modern Christian music, if you haven't already guessed! If you want to rattle my cage, then tell me that modern Christian music is no better than the pop music of the age, with no truth, no liturgy, and no respect. This modern hymn overflows, line after line, with solid truth on which you can build your life.

It's a hymn which sounds great when sung by a large congregation. I remember singing it with three thousand people who had gathered for the Evangelical Alliance Assembly. The conviction in the voices shook the ground. It's a favourite in the Spring Harvest Big Top Celebrations. The reality of Jesus' crucifixion struck deep when singing this hymn at Minehead. The dancers draped cloth over a simple wooden cross and the words rang in my head, 'Till on that cross as Jesus died, The wrath of God was satisfied. For every sin on Him was laid.'

* * *

My six weeks of radiotherapy came to a thankful end. I was so pleased not to have to drive to Brighton each day. Chemotherapy continued and should have carried on over Christmas into the New Year. The effects of the radiotherapy continue on after the treatment finishes. While I was sore in unmentionable places, that was bearable, but the extra radiotherapy I had on the area where the lymph gland had been removed caused the skin to burn unpleasantly. It was uncomfortable to wear cloth against my skin, but necessary when out in public! I experimented with various bandages but they always instantly fell off. As time went on, the skin wouldn't heal. I began to find it difficult to drive, unable comfortably to press down on the clutch. I felt like an old man hobbling around. The chemotherapy, which was killing off any new cells left, right and centre, was making it difficult for the skin to heal. It was decided that I would have a two-week break from treatment. I was stunned at how quickly things began to heal only a few days after coming off the drugs. It was a real wake up call to how powerful the drugs were and how much they were affecting me.

The two-week break coincided with the Christmas holidays and it felt great to walk out of the chemotherapy ward and not return for two weeks. I didn't have to worry about treatment over the holidays and didn't have to travel down to Eastbourne each week for the blood tests and pump changes. For the first time in four months I felt a free man. I was shown how to flush my own line. The plastic tubes had to be kept clean and so each week saline solution would be pumped through them to wash them out. It was a really odd sensation when I felt the cold solution enter the vein. The claves, or toggles, also had to be changed weekly. These were the plastic fastenings at the end of the tube which attached the tubes from the pump to the tubes entering my chest. I left for home with bags of syringes, tubes of saline solution and disinfectant.

That Christmas was a mixed bag of happiness and sadness. I was so pleased to be off treatment but knew that I would have to return to it. I had been looking forward to the end of treatment but now the goalposts had been moved so far back I could no longer see them.

The joy of being with my family in London was heightened because of what I'd been through, yet in the distance loomed the fearful reality of cancer. Would this be the last time? We had many visitors over the holidays, people I didn't see that often. It was so good to see people, yet there was the awkwardness about whether we should talk about cancer. In my life in Sussex I had got used to being open about my treatment and how I was feeling. The people around me there saw the good as well as the bad. The people I saw over Christmas were very dear to me but somehow in the pressure created by only being together for a few hours, knowing a lot of time would pass before we would see each other again, I found it hard to talk openly and preferred to avoid the whole subject. I found this difficult as I felt I wasn't able to be real with people and I wanted to be real.

I'm one of five. Add in a sister-in-law, two young nephews and Christmas becomes busy and fun. We try and hold onto the family Christmas traditions. While Father Christmas no longer leaves sacks of presents at the foot of the bed, complaining that the little children stay up too late these days, it is still traditional to open Father Christmas' presents before breakfast. Church is a funny mixture of presents and the Nativity and seeing people whom you haven't seen since last Christmas. Wine now joins the Shloer for the traditional Christmas dinner and the latest in cracker technology gives us various magic tricks which lead to hours of entertainment and 'How did you do that' gasps. The Queen's voice still controls what time the brothers and sisters will exchange their gifts, but she's now embroiled in controversy each year as the Royalists heatedly debate the pros and cons of the monarchy with the Republicans. Rum butter normally soothes any ill temper. The washing-up still adds an element of tension, and no, apparently having weeks of radiotherapy and chemotherapy is no excuse for not helping. All is soon forgotten under the mountain of wrapping paper and all that hinting pays off. If nephews are good enough they are allowed to watch as their toys are played with. Anne Robinson keeps showing up at our family Christmas with her wretched Weakest Link game. Fathers grumble as they are voted off in the first rounds, complaining that statistically they are not the weakest link and find solace in the pickled onion jar. Out comes the Bailey's and the day draws to a close.

I loved everything about the day but mixed in with my joy was a touch of loneliness. No one else in my family had cancer. This was not something we could share. We would all go our separate ways again but I was the one who had to return to chemotherapy, doctors, surgery, life or death. I didn't want to be different from my brothers and sisters. I didn't want to be the ill one. I wanted to be as healthy as they were. This made me feel lonely. In the weeks that followed I was hurt by the reality that my life was taking a different path from my siblings. I just didn't want to be different.

Jesus' arrival on earth is a strange tale. The Son of God was born in a stable, recognised by so few. God decided to bridge the gap between himself and his creation by becoming a part of it as a human. God as a baby? The joy of new birth but also the start of a journey leading to an awful death. It's magical story but an odd one.

Sometimes lost in this story is an incredible truth: God became man.

> In Christ alone, who took on flesh
> Fulness of God in helpless babe
> This gift of love and righteousness...

I believe in a mystery. Jesus Christ was both God and man; fully divine, fully human. If having a faith was just about choosing from a range of options a religion that you liked the sound of and fitted you comfortably, then I'd choose Christianity because of this simple fact, God became man. This is important to me because it shows the extent God is willing to go to identify with his creation. He knows what it is like to be human. He knows what it is like to enjoy life and he knows what it is like to struggle as a human being on this planet. He can identify with our joy, and our pain, our happiness and our struggles.

My identification with Jesus goes deeper than this.

> ...on that cross as Jesus died
> The wrath of God was satisfied
> For every sin on Him was laid

Jesus knew what it was like to live with a death sentence over him. What I had to face was in no way comparable to what Jesus went through. I only had to face the fact that I might die an early and uncomfortable death. He knew what lay before him, knew he would die young and painfully. Yet realising that Jesus lived with this knowledge throughout his life and could identify with my fears for the future brought me comfort. The loneliness I felt diminished as I realised that I didn't face it alone, or face it with someone who had never had to deal with such fears. Jesus became my comforter.

There was comfort also in the fact that Jesus' death had a purpose. It wasn't pointless and it fitted a grander plan.

* * *

In Christ alone my hope is found
He is my light, my strength, my song
This cornerstone, this solid ground
Firm through the fiercest drought and storm
What heights of love, what depths of peace
When fears are stilled, when strivings cease
My Comforter, my All in All
Here in the love of Christ I stand.

After Christmas it was decided that a new chemotherapy regimen was needed to reduce the tumour further. Instead of the 24/7 chemotherapy, I went in once every two weeks. My line stayed in permanently and this was attached to a drip that fed the drugs into me over a period of two to three hours. I then had a concoction of steroids and anti-sickness drugs injected to stop me feeling sick. Finally a pump was attached, similar to but larger than the one I had before and I wore this for 48 hours. These drugs were more intense than the previous ones and had their own set of side effects. My hair began to fall out. I did not lose all of it. In fact, to anybody else it wasn't noticeable as I had quite thick hair. In one sense it didn't bother me too much as I've often had most of my hair shaved off. However, I estimate I lost half of it. My pillow, my bath and my clothes would be covered with little hairs. When it was wet I could see my scalp, something I couldn't see before. I lost body hair as well. It wasn't the hair loss that scared me, it was the obvious changes in my body caused by the drugs.

Another side effect was that I really felt the cold. I thought they were being silly when I was instructed to come to my first chemotherapy appointment with gloves, scarf and woolly hat. But it was incredible. After a few hours of treatment the slightest hint of cold air made me freeze. What was so unusual was that my hands and feet responded dramatically to touching anything cold with painful pins and needles. Directly after the treatment and for the days I was on the pump, I was unable to touch anything cold without it hurting. I couldn't put my hand in the freezer at all and could only get things out of the fridge with thick gloves on. I did keep forgetting at first so Rachel put a sign on the fridge to remind me. I kept thinking, I can bear it for a moment, but it really hurt. I also could not cope with cold drinks. Even tap water would make my throat feel as if it was closing up and I couldn't breathe. It wasn't closing but it was a very unpleasant sensation. If I ever got cold because I wasn't wearing enough layers, my body reacted dramatically. I would shiver so much I couldn't operate and the only solution would be to pile blankets on top of me but it would take a long time to warm up. I had to be very careful when showering to make sure the water was the right temperature. The effects were less dramatic when I wasn't connected to the pump. I could drink a cold drink as long as I wrapped something round the cup to protect my hands and sipped it slowly.

My appetite also changed. I was told the drugs could affect my hormones in the same way pregnancy affects women's hormones. I found that at certain times I had no appetite at all, then I would crave something a bit odd. For one meal all I could face was peas so I ate two bowlfuls. Other times I could eat for England. With hot flushes, cold spells and a strange appetite, I began to feel menopausal.

The side effect that I struggled with the most was the incredible tiredness. I had the treatment on Mondays, was fine on Tuesday and Wednesday but come Thursday I would begin to feel rough. By Friday evening I would be exhausted and unable to do anything. Saturday would be similar but by Sunday I was on the up again. The following week I would be absolutely fine, although I had to be careful. Then it would begin again. It seemed to get harder to face and harder to live with each time. Originally I was to have four cycles of treatment. This was extended to six. I found it increasingly difficult to psych myself up for it each Monday. The treatment before Christmas did make me tired but it was nothing compared to the new regimen. This was a new kind of tiredness which made my mind as well as my body tired.

The Friday evenings and Saturdays were always the worst. I would drag myself out of bed but spend the whole day on the sofa and sometimes go back to bed and sleep from 7pm all through the night. I found it tiring to watch TV, impossible to concentrate on a book, and at times I couldn't even speak on the phone because my brain couldn't put together a coherent sentence.

To realise that a drug was affecting not only my body but my mind was scary. I wondered if it was doing permanent damage. Would there be one time too many and I wouldn't recover from it? It made me feel old as I couldn't do anything. I had to plan my days carefully knowing I only had a few hours of activity in me. Again I wondered would I end up stuck in this state, would I be old before my time? There was also something so horrid about feeling okay but having to go into the hospital knowing that the drugs would start the cycle again. I had a choice and could escape the cycle, but the alternative was far worse.

If this is how I felt, I dread to think what it is like for those who have to go in and stay in hospital for their chemotherapy because it makes them so sick that they can't operate. How they prepare themselves to face it time and time again, I do not know. That's true bravery, to get into that hospital bed, be connected and then live through the days of sickness, get up and then do it all over again.

The aim of this treatment was to reduce the size of the tumour to a size small enough to operate on and remove. The first months of treatment had not reduced it significantly. It did respond as time went on. However, while everybody was pleased when it began to shrink, I found I couldn't share the optimism. The fact that it was getting smaller brought the operation nearer. I know it was foolish but I secretly hoped it wouldn't get smaller. Despite the side effects of the drugs, they still seemed preferable to surgery.

Everybody remained so supportive. One small act of kindness meant so much to me. On a chemotherapy day I would be attached to the drip around 2pm. This was the time the tea guy did his rounds. From then on it was self-service. I didn't find it easy to wheel my drip machine across the ward carrying a cup of tea. Sometimes I had two machines attached and moving at all was more trouble than it was worth. A few hours in and I would want a cup of tea but not quite enough to risk movement. The mother from someone in my church had cancer and at that point was coming in on Monday afternoons for her chemotherapy pump change. Each week she would make me a cup of tea while waiting for the nurse and ask how I was doing. It made such a difference to how I felt.

I returned to work after Christmas and with a lot of flexibility on Spring Harvest's part, I was able to do a few more days. While I wouldn't admit it then, I did overdo it a bit and was told off more than once for rushing to appointments and falling asleep during chemotherapy. I even fell asleep in the MRI scanner tube on one occasion;

most odd waking up in it! I don't know why I ever rushed to any appointment. I was hurrying down the main corridor of Eastbourne Hospital one day and felt an arm block my way. It was my oncologist wondering why I was rushing. She admitted that she was never on time with her appointments so why was I tiring myself out to be on time? I don't know why but I always felt that I should be on time and that if I missed an appointment slot I would be put to the back of the queue and have to wait till the end of the day to be seen. It isn't like that of course but you still feel you have to be on time. Yet despite all that happened I found I couldn't cut a work phone conversation off with, 'I have to go, I've got chemotherapy' and so would forever find myself speeding down the A22 from Uckfield to Eastbourne. However, after a few stern words, I worked out with my oncologist what days could be work days and what should be rest days when I wouldn't work, no matter how I felt.

Life fell into some sort of order, although I found it hard to say no to social invitations and things I wanted to do and so at times life was a hectic mix of work, play and treatment. I started going out with a girl who didn't live locally and somehow we fitted in a few weekends together, with a fair bit of travelling. Life was very full. I was daft to try and fit so much into an existence that involved such full-on treatment, but I couldn't give up my life that easily. I didn't want to give in to the cancer and let it spoil everything. I also didn't want to give in because secretly I feared that any change to my life would be another step towards first losing my health, second my independence and ultimately my life.

A few days in hospital slowed me down somewhat. I had been having a pain in my chest and wondered if the drugs were weakening my heart. So did the hospital staff.

I was naughty and left it a while. I did have a defence for why I waited. I didn't want a fuss made and always felt I was wasting everyone's time. At a Sunday evening meeting at church, I struggled to sit upright. Both Andy and Rachel told me I had to say something and were all for taking me to the hospital there and then. I managed to negotiate leaving it until the next day, my chemotherapy day, when I promised to tell the nurses.

I didn't tell them at first. But as the pains started coming while I was having treatment so I felt it was time to own up. In a flurry of activity I was disconnected from the drips, put on a bed and attached to an ECG machine. There I remained for the rest of the afternoon and evening. As is always the case with me, the pains didn't come back at the intensity that I had first experienced. I felt I was making a fuss and I'd be okay. The staff didn't agree. I was put in a wheelchair and pushed off for an x-ray. I felt so silly, dressed in my work clothes, being pushed down the corridor. I said I was fine to walk but was told I wasn't allowed. I was left in the queue in the x-ray department. My chair was in the way so I got up and moved it. I was sternly told not to get out of my chair, I had been put in it for a reason and I should ask for help if I needed to move, otherwise I should keep still. I was surrounded by old ladies in their nighties down from the wards, all looking a good deal frailer than me. I kept expecting a passerby to tell me off for taking up a much needed wheelchair.

The x-rays and ECGs didn't really show anything. They decided to keep me in for observation. They only had a private room free, so to my delight I ended up with my own room with TV, DVD, video, phone and bathroom. I knew I was tired when again I realised I was happy to stay overnight in a hospital. There is such a relief in these situations in switching off and letting someone else look after you. I had regular ECGs but they didn't show anything. I was given an emergency pull cord in case the pains came. At one point I rolled over it and set it off accidentally and was surprised when a nurse burst in. It was all rather dramatic and I felt a complete fraud.

I was seen by a cardio specialist. It was one of those horrible occasions where the doctor is accompanied by an army of trainee doctors. You want to say 'No' when they ask if it's okay if the consultation is observed but you know that they have to learn somehow and have seen far worse so you say 'Yes' and die slowly of embarrassment. He declared my heart fit and active. I was discharged. After a bit of debate it was thought that the pains were caused by my chemotherapy drugs. One of the drugs was a new type and another patient had a similar experience. It was decided to reduce the drugs, taking me off the one which caused the cold extremities and hair loss. From that point on the chemotherapy did get easier to cope with. My rate of hair loss decreased and I was a lot less tired.

Despite the relief of coming off the drug I was concerned that this would affect the success of the treatment. I said I would prefer to stay on the treatment and live with the side effects if it meant I had a higher chance of beating the cancer. This is the difficult thing about chemotherapy. They have to weigh up the benefits of the treatment with the effect on the body. While it could have a positive effect on the tumour it could be damaging other parts. I learnt also that with chemotherapy there are no definite answers. They do not know if the treatment will work. The medical situation began to feel hopeless and what I had begun to understand about God, about healing, about my destiny began to be tested by the reality that the disease was not giving up easily.

The words of this song gave me comfort and helped me focus on the truth that I knew about God. I believed in eternal life. After my death I was going to heaven. I didn't fully grasp what heaven would be but I believed there I would be with God, the Creator of both heaven and earth. I understood how my sin stood in the way. More than just the sum of all my wrongdoings, my very nature is steeped in sin. I was born into a sinful world that rejects God, day in day out, and this affected everything about me. I was cursed in sin. God in all his holiness, his righteousness and his justice couldn't ignore sin. It had to be dealt with, punished. He chose to take that punishment himself and so sent his Son Jesus who, when crucified, took on the punishment for all my wrongdoing and removed the very thing that meant I couldn't come close to God. I believed that 'the wrath of God was satisfied' because 'every sin on Him was laid'. He paid the ultimate price by taking my punishment. Jesus didn't stay dead. *He rose again.* Jesus defeated death, he defeated the curse of sin over me.

I realised, when going over these words, how confusing they must seem to some people. They may sound like I have been indoctrinated, the words repeated in parrot-like fashion. I have spent years trying to understand heaven, hell, sin, judgement, redemption. I still find I am unwrapping this mystery, trying to understand, trying to explain. Yet I do believe it. My hope in doctors and treatments was not secure. As I sang this hymn eternal truths burned in my heart. I didn't understand it all, I didn't have an in-depth theological knowledge that made me sure. My faith brought it to life inside me.

As He stands in victory
Sin's curse has lost its grip on me
For I am His and He is mine
Bought with the precious blood of Christ

I had given my life to God when I chose to be a Christian. This song helped me realise an amazing truth; sin's curse was defeated and its grip on me crushed. I was no ordinary person; I had been bought. I belonged to God and, mystery of all mystery, he belonged to me.

This belief involved a step of faith but it directly affected the reality of my life. I felt I had lost control over my destiny. I felt cancer was a curse over me that would lead to my defeat. This song reminded me that I didn't control my destiny because I had chosen to leave it in God's hands. I had said countless times before, 'You are my God and I will submit to you.' I meant it, I just forgot in the humdrum of life that God didn't want my life so that he could bottle it. He wanted to use it, he had plans for it, he had a purpose. This was beyond the reach of death or the curse of sin because he had defeated it.

No guilt in life, no fear in death
This is the power of Christ in me
From life's first cry to final breath
Jesus commands my destiny
No power of hell, no scheme of man
Can ever pluck me from His hand
Till He returns or calls me home
Here in the power of Christ I'll stand.

I cried so often when I sang this song because as I sang it, I realised it was true. I did not need to live a life of guilt. I did not need to fear death. Cancer couldn't finish me off, nothing from this world or from hell could take me from God. I could rest secure in God's hands.

This was the hope that the treatment could not provide. I wish I had the skill to put it into words easier to understand. I wish I could explain the theology which surrounds each line of this song. I wish you could come inside my head and feel the emotional and physical reaction when I sing the line 'I am His and He is Mine.'

* * *

At that stage I did not know if I would survive cancer. My hope wasn't being placed in God healing me of cancer. Others believed that I was going to be healed and that a long life lay ahead of me. I didn't know if God would heal me or not. But I realised that it didn't ultimately matter either way. The song doesn't say we live for ever on this earth, it says 'from life's first cry to final breath'. God raised my eyes above the reality of this life to a greater eternal reality. He showed me again the healing which was guaranteed. Cancer would not finish me. Every sorrow, every pain, every hurt had been healed in the light of eternity. I would be whole, perfect and healed. This had been made possible by Jesus' death.

He defeated every consequence of sin, illness, pain, and the ultimate, death itself.

Here in the power of Christ I'll stand.

Note

1   Stuart Townend and Keith Getty, *In Christ Alone* (© 2001 Thankyou Music)

9. That's What's So Amazing about Your Grace[1]

As quickly as treatment started, it finished. I had the sixth and final session on the Monday and after my 48 hours on the pump I was finally disconnected and my line taken out. I'm not squeamish and so was fascinated watching the line coming out. For months I'd had to be extra careful as any heavy lifting or awkward movements could pull it out. There was a little cuff round the line which went just under the skin to hold it in place. This had half come out, showing how much had already been pulled. One quick tug and out it came. I felt it go, a most odd sensation. It felt so good not to have it any more. I had to wait for the stitch to come out but after that I stood under the shower and let the water pour over me. For the first time in months I no longer had to worry about not getting anything wet.

A week later I went to Spring Harvest 2003 in Minehead. I kept expecting something to happen that would mean I wouldn't be able to go. Someone would decide that I needed some other treatment. I was just waiting for that wretched boil to return or some other problem to arise. For months I'd worried that I would be left behind while all my workmates got stuck into the fun and the challenges which we at Spring Harvest call simply, site. Suddenly it was upon us and the doctors were saying I could go and didn't have to go anywhere near a hospital for six weeks.

I wanted a bit of normality and as crazy as this may sound to anybody involved in the behind-the-scenes running of Spring Harvest, I knew that I could find it on site. I knew people would either not know that I had cancer or would be too busy to focus on it. I was able to talk to my boss about my feelings about going to the event and, other than the fact I wasn't to be involved in anything too physical, I was to be a normal member of the team. I was to keep a low profile when heavy physical help was needed so that I wouldn't have to explain why a perfectly healthy looking male was standing by while everyone else did the hard stuff. I wasn't to go anywhere near a lorry. Of course I was gutted not to be loading lorries, to be denied this pleasure. The thought of all my colleagues straining with box after box without me there to lend a hand... how would they cope without me! It was decided that some people would be asked to pray for me and another member of our staff who had cancer, but names wouldn't be given. I wanted to leave cancer behind and to be normal, and in the extremely long days and hard work of the main event, I found that normality.

I am unashamedly proud of Spring Harvest. It is an extraordinary event. It is the largest Christian gathering in Europe and takes place at two large Butlins' sites in Minehead and Skegness. Christians from many backgrounds get together, worship and learn together. So many differences are set aside. The teaching is Bible-based and cutting edge. At the 2003 event I felt there was a return to times of worship which had characterised Spring Harvest celebrations of the past and which reached deep into the hearts of people like me who love to worship God in song.

There is a danger in regarding yearly conferences as a spiritual fill-up at the heavenly garage, necessary to keep going for another year. However, it has been my experience that God uses times away from my normal life to teach me new things and equip me for when I go back. It's not that he can't and doesn't speak to me in daily life, it's just sometimes he wants to take me aside for something special. I'll steal a phrase from my friend George, 'Spring Harvest rocks.' It doesn't rock because it's big, it doesn't rock because Butlins' sites are so great for holidays. It doesn't rock because the speakers are good, the bands up to date and exciting. It rocks because God works through it to changes lives, to challenge, to build and year after year people meet him there and are affected.

For the best part of three weeks cancer was forgotten. Not entirely. I was watching the morning Bible Reading and the preacher was speaking about being angry. He said it was okay to be angry with God, he was big enough to take it. I don't know if it was the fact that we were coming to the end of the final week and the reality of cancer was pushing its way back into my thoughts, but suddenly I was angry. Before, I was angry with myself, this time I was angry with God. I raged at him. It just wasn't fair. It wasn't fair that I had cancer. It wasn't fair that he hadn't ripped open the roof of the Big Top and asked to see me to deal with my situation. Why did I have an old man's disease at a young age? Why was I single at the age of thirty and not happily married with 2.4 children? Why did I not have the financial security that I expected at this age? The list of 'why nots' went on for some time. I hoped the speaker was right about it being okay to be angry with God because I was flipping mad at him!

After listening to the morning Bible Reading I was supposed to be going to play Laser Quest with my colleagues. It was a thank you treat for the efforts put in over the long three weeks. I didn't dare go. I didn't want to point imaginary lasers at people, I wanted to smash a rifle butt over the head of anyone who was foolish enough to come anywhere near me. I wanted to get the anger and pain out of me and into someone else. Fortunately for my colleagues, I chose not to go.

God didn't come down to fight me and put me in my place. He didn't send anyone to comfort me. Nor did he send his dove of peace to calm me. A bit of self control and a cry on the beach had to suffice and I returned to work and the anger passed. God has an amazing fatherly nature and he is willing to let us thrash out our tantrums and to let us chuck all our rubbish in his direction and still be there with arms open wide to give us a cuddle.

* * *

Just before we had left for site I had decided that I needed some time out. I needed to stop work, take a break and try and come to some kind of understanding of what was going on with my life. I had decided that I wanted to try to write about my experiences and I knew that I needed time to do it properly. I asked for and was granted a sabbatical. I was so tired after Spring Harvest that I knew I had to stop or I was going to do myself some harm. The doctors were more than happy to sign me off work. I think I heard a sigh of relief! Everyone was in agreement, I needed a rest after chemotherapy and the events of the past months. I was feeling quite good physically but realised that the treatment had taken away a lot of my stamina. The smallest physical thing was tiring me out. It was time to stop.

A few days after returning home I went for a short walk on the Sussex Downs. It was a gorgeous sunny day, spring was turning to summer. It felt great to look forward to four months off, come what may medically. For some reason I began to think about the relationship between sin and sickness while wandering along. It was a difficult subject and I found myself debating various issues in my head. On one hand I could see the reality that involvement in some sin led to sickness. It said in the Bible that sleeping around was a sin. AIDS was a sexually transmitted disease. The sin could lead to contracting the illness. I didn't feel that AIDS was a punishment from God because of the person's sin. I concluded that in some cases the sickness could be a consequence of doing something God said not to do. On the other hand I could not say this was always the case. To a child born with a disabling condition, I could not say your sin caused your illness. I remembered the story in John 9 where Jesus did not attribute the blindness of a man blind from birth to his or his parents' sin. Despite not being able to form a definite argument, I didn't feel entirely innocent and able to say that my sin played no role in my becoming sick.

A few months earlier I had tackled this issue when talking with Andy. Maybe out of the emotional intensity of being seriously ill, I had not wanted to leave any stone unturned in trying to understand and deal with my situation. I was aware that God was working in my life, knocking down and rebuilding. I wanted to respond to the God who had been my rock by ensuring I was living right. I wanted to tackle sin in my life head on. It felt as if God was bringing past actions, as well as on-going issues, into the spotlight for me to deal with. Andy acted as my priest, heard my confessions and helped me ask God for forgiveness. It was a powerful time which allowed God to work at a deep level and set me free from the strongholds I had allowed into my life. It was the first step in which God began a powerful healing of greater significance than the healing of my body.

As I was walking along the South Downs path, holding this debate in my head, I considered my character. I was a sinner. I did wrong things. Why should I have got away with them and expected to live a long healthy life while others got punished for their sins with sickness? And there didn't seem to be any scale. Big sins didn't lead to big illnesses. Murderers didn't necessarily get cancer and die any more than people who have never broken the law escaped cancer. It seemed too random to draw any clear conclusions. Yes, some activity leads to certain illnesses, but mostly it appeared to be a random sample of people who contract serious illnesses. Sickness couldn't be a punishment from God. If it was purely about sin, why were some punished and others not? Despite all these questions I knew where I stood, a sinner through and through.

My thinking progressed a bit. I contemplated the link between sickness and the sinful state of the world. When Adam and Eve started the sin stuff, sickness came into the world. While it seemed random, who fell ill and who didn't, I could see a link between the world being sinful and there being so much sickness in it.

I allowed myself to think along the lines that God could be punishing me for my sin by giving me cancer. I came to an unpleasant conclusion. If God said I deserved to die for my sin then who was I to claim I was innocent and it was all unfair? If my sin was so great that I deserved to die then die I should. I couldn't deny that I was a sinner and if God felt the world would be a better place without me then I had no choice but to accept the punishment. It hit me hard. I did deserve to die. If sin is what separated me from God, God who is the Creator and very Sustainer of all life, then I was a sinner and separated from God.

Another thought struck me. While I deserved to die, so did everyone else. I wasn't unique. Everyone else had sinned, everyone was also separated from God. Forget a scale of big to little sins, the Bible said that all sin leads to death, leads to separation from God. I wasn't noticing newborn lambs prancing around the downland fields in the sun at that point. It was a sobering moment.

It was at that exact moment that a line from a song I had heard for the first time at Spring Harvest 2003 went through my mind.

That's what's so amazing about your grace.

Suddenly I understood a word I had heard so many times but never quite got. I understood grace. I actually laughed out loud, sending lambs scampering across the fields. I deserved to die, we all did, but that was not what God wanted and he had provided a solution. The ultimate penalty for my sin was taken for me by Jesus. He died to take my punishment. Yes, I had come to realise this, as the previous chapter has shown, but suddenly the sheer grace of God hit me. I deserved to die but I didn't have to because Someone had stood in my place. I was reminded of a song line which strangely I had woken up with in my head on many a morning:

Be glad, for every debt that you ever had
Has been paid up in full by the grace of the Lord
Be glad, be glad, be glad.[2]

Again God raised my eyes above all the debate over the nature of sin and its relationship to sickness and showed me a far greater eternal truth. Regardless of whether my sickness was caused by my sin, my parents' sin, or the sins of all humanity, the answer was still the same.

For God so loved the world that he gave his one and only Son, that whoever believes in him shall not perish but have eternal life. For God did not send his Son into the world to condemn the world, but to save the world through him.

(John 3:16–17)

I had confessed my sin before, but at that point I understood what grace God had shown me by forgiving me. A year later at Spring Harvest 2004, our theme was *Grace Academy*. We sang many songs centring on God's grace but the most popular was the hymn *Amazing Grace*. I could experience both the sobering awareness of the 'wretch' I was, and the indescribable joy of knowing I was saved, the price paid; I was twice God's, created by him and bought by his grace.

* * *

So lift your eyes to the things as yet unseen.[3]

I do see a direct link with salvation and healing. I'm saved now, I receive grace now, but I still remain in this world of sin. I still live surrounded by the consequence of a fallen world. I must play my part in bringing good to this world now, while I can. But my heart longs for heaven. I long for the eternity with God that my salvation promises. I long for liberation from the evil of this world. I believe it will come.

> There is a day that all creation's waiting for
> A day of freedom and liberation from the earth
> And on that day the Lord will come to meet His bride
> And when we see Him in an instant we'll be changed.
>
> The trumpet sounds and the dead will then be raised
> By His power never to perish again
> Once only flesh now clothed with immortality
> Death has now been swallowed up in victory.

I long for death to be swallowed up in victory. The curse of death has been broken, death is no longer separation from God. But the story is not yet over. I'm still living surrounded by death. Again God lifts my eyes above the current circumstances and tells me to look to the future. What is around me isn't everything. The eternal reality is a world where we will be liberated, we will not perish again.

> We will meet Him in the air and then we will be like Him
> For we will see Him as He is…
> Then all hurt and pain will cease and we'll be with Him
>   forever
> And in His glory we will live.

I've already said that I don't know why some people are healed and others aren't. But what I am sure of, beyond a doubt, is that sickness is not the end. We will meet Jesus, we will be changed, hurt and pain will cease. By the grace of God, through Jesus' death, sickness has been dealt with. It cannot separate us from God. Understanding this fact led to an amazing healing of my heart. It has enabled people I have seen die, die in victory for they knew their healing was secure, they would be whole with God. Does he heal everybody's actual physical illnesses here on earth before they die? I have to say no. Why? I can't answer, but I can direct people's eyes higher.

I came to this understanding before I went somewhere to pursue a healing for my body. God had started a spiritual healing work in me. I don't know if I can look a dying person in the eye and say 'Look up.' I've not had to do it. Despite what I've been through I have no real experience of death. I haven't lost a loved one to a horrible illness. My understanding of death remains in the hypothetical, the 'what could have been', not in what has happened. However, I feel compelled to write what I feel I have learnt, in the hope it will be of value.

So lift your eyes to the things as yet unseen
That will remain now for all eternity
Though trouble's hard it's only momentary
And it's achieving our future glory

Notes

1 Matt Redman, *A Love So Undeserved (Amazing)* (© 2002 Thankyou
   Music)
2 Michael Kelly Blanchard, *Be Ye Glad* (© 1988 Paragon Music Corp/
   Benson Music Group Inc.)
3 Nathan Fellingham, *There Is A Day* (© 2001 Thankyou Music)

10. You're King and You Reign over all Things[1]

The first month of my so-called sabbatical wasn't as quiet and restful as it was at first intended to be.

After returning from Spring Harvest I headed off with my friend Paul to his parents' place in Provence. There I did manage to catch up on some rest, mainly by their lovely outdoor pool in the sun. I love France. I'm not sure what I love more, the quieter pace of life or the food. You can't beat combining the two in a long leisurely lunch of bread, cheese and of course the obligatory glass or two of red.

I returned to England for a quick round of scans and appointments before heading back to Gatwick and jumping on a plane bound again for France. Spring Harvest were opening their new Spring Harvest Holidays campsite in the Vendée on the west coast of France. I spent a busy, if very wet, weekend helping with the final push to get the place ready. There were hundreds of sets of plastic garden furniture to be put together and the team set to work. An hour of manual work was enough to send me to my bed so I focused on the important task of preparing lunch for everyone. I was in seventh heaven hacking at French bread, slicing cheese and chopping salad. Shopping with a company credit card and no defined budget was such fun. I had been to the campsite a year before just a few weeks after it was bought. Returning a year later the transformation was very noticeable. It's a lovely place, well worth a holiday visit.

My mid-French holidays appointment was with a cancer specialist at St Mark's Hospital in London. For some time I had been considering having a second opinion but it was a difficult decision to make. While I was entitled to one, I couldn't help but worry that it might annoy my own specialist. However, I didn't want to miss any opportunity to avoid surgery. My scans had been showing that the tumour had shrunk further and it looked as if it would soon be time to face the knife. At one point the possibility of having a reversible operation was discussed. The bowel would be removed and a stoma created. I would have to have a colostomy bag but after time it might be possible to have another operation and put everything back to how it should be. It seemed much easier to face the possibility of a temporary colostomy. But there was a further complication; another lymph gland was showing signs of swelling. If it was cancerous, then again it had spread to the lymph system. Once there it could spread around the body. I was glad when my Eastbourne doctors decided a second opinion was needed and I was sent to London.

I saw a professor and he spoke clearly and explained things well. He repeated that my case was an unusual one. He gave what he thought were the three possible courses of action which would depend on the condition of the tumour.

Firstly, he said that if the cancer had spread to the lymph system then there would be no point in operating to remove the bowel. It would be too late to close the stable door, the horse had bolted. It would spread and attack other organs. If this was the case he said that I should have further chemotherapy. He was direct. He said that this would be the worst-case scenario. The chemotherapy would only be able to contain the cancer for a time; it would not get rid of it.

Secondly, if the scan showed that there was cancer in the bowel but it had not spread further he recommended surgery. In addition to taking out the bowel they would take out many of the lymph glands in the area. As the cancer had already spread once to a gland, others would be taken out to reduce the risk of it happening again. The consequence of this would be loss of urinary and sexual function and I would need both a colostomy and a catheter. The operation would be irreversible.

Thirdly, if there was no sign of any cancer in either the bowel or lymph system, he would still recommend the surgery. He said that in the majority of cases where the original cancer had spread as far as mine, it would return. The statistics he gave me were similar to those I had heard before. If I didn't have an operation to remove the bowel, there was an 80 per cent chance the cancer would return. If I had the operation, there was a 70 per cent chance the cancer would return. The operation would offer a 10 per cent additional chance of keeping the cancer at bay. In short, he would recommend surgery because he would expect the cancer to return and the best thing to do would be to remove the organ which was first affected.

I left wondering where was the good option? Where was the option that my treatment had worked, there was no cancer and no surgery was needed? How could these three options with their dire consequences be all I had?

Two days later I had what is called a PET scan. It was the most powerful scan, giving the finest picture of what was going on. This was the scan that would help determine which course of action lay ahead. For the PET scan I was injected with a radioactive dye which came in a small syringe encased within a larger plastic tube, all of which arrived in a sealed metal box. It was a little dramatic and I couldn't help but wonder what on earth they were injecting into me. The nurses who work surrounded by these dangerous radioactive drugs have to wear bleepers which go off when they are in the proximity of either the drugs or a person who has the drugs in their system. It was amusing to walk down the corridors setting off bleepers as I went. They would begin bleeping quietly as I approached but build up to a louder, faster warning as I drew close. I was radioactive! When I told Mark about the bleepers he insisted that they had nothing to do with the radioactive drugs but were the latest in nurse protection, a device to warn them when trouble was approaching! The scanning machine was similar to an MRI machine although my head stuck out the other end. I had to keep still for two sessions of 45 minutes. By then I was a pro at dozing off but annoyingly I kept being woken by an advert on the radio in which a wife called her husband who wasn't responding. The guy was called John. I kept hearing 'John, John, JOHN, JOHN!' and would wake thinking the nurses were trying to get my attention. Thankfully I didn't move too much and avoided having to repeat the 45-minute scan.

A day later and I was on a plane heading back to France, slightly dazed at how different one day could be from the next; one day radioactive man, the next an international traveller.

* * *

For the next bit of the story we have to take a big step back to the previous September. Andy had received a letter saying that I should go to The Synagogue of All Nations in Lagos, Nigeria. The Synagogue was in fact a church and there were various reports of people being healed there. God was working through a guy called TB Joshua and people were being healed by the hundreds; week in, week out. At that point Andy was filtering such letters for me. I was not in a place where I could cope with people making suggestions of what I should do, where I should go. Talk of going anywhere for God to heal me confused and hurt me. Andy prayerfully considered the letter but felt it was not right to pass it on to me. He prayed that if it was right for me to go a way would open up at the right time.

I had heard of this church before. A colleague, Trine, had been there and was amazingly healed. She had been into work and said what had happened to her. Her story buzzed around the office. I had missed her visit to the office but what I heard scared me. I didn't understand it, wasn't able to make a rational decision as to whether I should go. To be blunt, I didn't want anything to do with it. I didn't want to meet Trine and talk about it. I didn't want to enter into discussion. I knew God could heal me but didn't want to consider having to go anywhere for him to do it.

The week before I went to Minehead in April I was invited to join a group that was to be going out to Lagos in June. Someone had offered to cover all expenses. At first I experienced my typical reaction. I didn't want to go, didn't understand why I needed to go there to be healed, but was fearful of missing any opportunity for God to heal me. I decided not to make a decision at that point. I wanted my dose of normality. I wanted to forget cancer and throw myself into Spring Harvest.

I did have an opportunity to talk to Trine and her husband when they were with us in Minehead. They were honest and direct about what took place in Lagos. It was clear from what they said that this was not a cult organisation practising strange magic. I had been fearful that the place was full of loonies and as soon as I was there I would be expected to do things I didn't want to do, and to believe things I didn't believe. I feared manipulation and I kept coming back to the same question, why did I have to go away to be healed? They explained that you were not forced to do anything while you were there. You observed the life of the church and, if you wished to, you could join the weekly prayer line where the sick were prayed for. Trine and Philip didn't seem like cult members brainwashed by some crazed maniac. I began to feel it would be okay to go.

Maybe I should have made one on-the-spot decision and stuck with it. Instead, the month that followed in the lead-up to the trip tore me apart. As I bounced between holidays, doctors' appointments and attempting to try and rest a bit, I fought to find what God wanted me to do. The options given by the professor at St Mark's were so dire that I was almost ready to try anything. I argued with myself that no matter what they did to me in Lagos it couldn't be worse than what the doctors planned in England. This wasn't enough to bring me peace on the matter. I worked my way through all the things that I had learnt. God was so clearly working through my circumstances. Should I go and see what happened or wait and see what he had planned for me?

This is one of the tensions I find a lot in my Christian life. Should I wait for God to act or should I get out there and do certain things that are necessary for God to work? Do I make choices and act or wait until I'm sure of God's direction? My thinking led me back to the broad path of God's will I had learnt about at the conference in November. I decided to trust that God wasn't going to sit in judgement over my decision to go. I didn't feel that God was definitely telling me to go to Lagos and if I went I would be healed but if I didn't, I'd miss being healed and have to face surgery, maybe even death. Nor did I feel he was telling me not to go and if I disobeyed, terrible consequences lay before me in Lagos; I would be forcibly inducted into a cult, misled, and open myself to some nasty stuff. God couldn't be this cruel judge sitting on his throne with a big stick and carrot, rewarding or punishing me depending on the choice I made. My God was a Father who loved me and wanted the best for me. I returned to the 'but this I know' things I had learnt, remembering the broad path of God's will and decided to go. I began to make plans.

Having made this decision my attention was then drawn to various websites with page after page of damning indictments against the church and its leader. These pages questioned TB Joshua's teaching and his salvation. Some denied miracles were happening. Other reports said that the miracles were happening but that it was not God who was at work, implying that demonic activity was taking place. As with all other reported moves of God, Toronto, Pensacola, Holy Trinity Brompton, there was an enormous amount of controversy.

I am not going to outline why some people believe that TB Joshua is not a Christian and that what happens in his church is of Satan, not of God. All you need to do is type in TB Joshua into an Internet search engine and you'll be amazed at the amount of stuff that comes up. All I'll say is that reading these pages tore me apart. I now not only feared that I could be going to a place full of nutters, I feared I could be going to a place under Satan's control and that I could be putting myself in a dangerous position. I began to question my decision to go.

People around me divided into two camps, those for and those against my trip. I was confused and stuck in the middle and felt no peace about the decision at all. On one hand I had the evidence of someone who had been there and the backing of my pastor, friends and colleagues. There was also the original letter from September. It had been put aside but now a way to go had appeared to open, as Andy had prayed. On the other hand, I had warnings that this was not a good man to see, and that it was a dangerous place to go. I did not hear directly from God either way.

I made my final decision based on three things. Firstly, those in the pro camp included people who had been and had first-hand knowledge of what was going on in Lagos. In addition to Trine and her husband, my father was able to talk to someone we both knew and respected who had been and said that this man was of God. Those who said no, and those who wrote the websites, had not been there and they did not have first-hand experience. Secondly, I focused on how I made my first decision to go. I held on to my belief that God allows us to make many choices but that he would be clear if there was something I should not do. I did not believe he was distant and waiting for me to mess up so he could come down and smite me. He had not given me a clear indication not to go. I believed I was in relationship with him, that he cared deeply for me and that he would not let me accidentally stray away from him into harm's way. If it was a dodgy place he would protect me. I trusted that his Spirit, who was in me, would guide me into truth and away from danger. Thirdly, I had a large group of people supporting me and praying for me. Would God ignore these prayers and hand me over to evil forces? Andy said something that made me smile but which reminded me of all those praying for me. One of the web pages contained a second-hand report of a lady who claimed she was held against her will at The Synagogue. Andy said that if they tried to kidnap me a group could mount a rescue mission. I thought about the people, who prayed for me, all deciding to go out to Lagos to get me. It would be quite a formidable group. There would be people coming from across the country and round the globe. At the forefront would be my family and friends. To be honest, you should see some of the older ladies who prayed for me from my London and Sussex churches. They alone, handbags in hand, could break me out of anywhere!

The amazing thing is I'm not exaggerating. The support a Christian can receive in their time of trouble can be immense. Thousands of people prayed for me.

> Over the invisible, over the visible, over all powers and
>   kingdoms
> You're King and You reign over all.

Making the decision tested me deeply but I trusted God had a course of action planned and put my faith in the fact that he, and no other power, reigned over everything, in Lagos and in the UK. I went.

Note

1 Geraldine Latty and Carey Luce, *You're King And You Reign Over All Things* (© 2003 Thankyou Music)

11. Who is Like my Jesus?

I chose this song lyric because it comes from a song I heard first on the bus from the airport, and then again and again in the church in Lagos. By the end of my week there I too was singing it with the same sense of amazement captured in the African lilt to the song: 'Who indeed is like my Jesus?'

From the moment I walked into the terminal building, with its heat and damp, slightly mouldy smell, I knew I was back in Africa. Memories of the sights, sounds and scents came flooding back from my time in the Comores. There is much I love about Africa but I'm afraid its cities are not my favourite. The journey to the church took us through some very run down areas. Most of the roads were dirt tracks winding past scruffy buildings. What was so noticeable was that there were churches everywhere with some unusual and long names. The Synagogue Church of All Nations seems tame compared to some we saw. There were billboards all over, advertising revival meetings and preaching sessions, showing smart African pastors in dark suits. If these didn't tell you that you were in a Christian part of the city then the shop names helped. I saw 'The King's Grocery Store', 'Christ's Hairdressers', 'Hosanna Internet café' and many more.

Right in the heart of this high-density suburb was an enormous building towering over everything else. Since Trine's last visit back in September the church building she had been in had been taken down and an enormous structure built. The proportions were large by UK standards and extraordinary by African. We estimated the new auditorium could hold twenty thousand people. I think somebody said the floor space was equivalent to three football pitches. Certainly one of our Spring Harvest Big Tops could easily have fitted in it with space to spare. It was not so much the size that amazed me, it was the fact that the church members had built it themselves and in such a short period of time. The only outside contractors involved had made the vast roofing beams but even these had been hoisted into place by the army of church members. It was an incredible achievement. With the roof on, attention was turning towards the interior decoration. There was a lot still to do but work was continuing at a cracking pace. Each window was engraved with a picture and Bible passage. These were being produced by some resident church artists who worked night and day in a corner of the building. No matter what time of day I went into the auditorium somebody was always working away at something.

The church was in a large compound. Outside there were covered areas where Sunday school classes and various church activities took place. There was a large dining room being built where members of the thirty-thousand strong congregation were able to get dinner. Various workshops produced the components needed for the building. One whole section was devoted to making each individual brick. Thousand upon thousand of metal chairs were being cast, covered and stacked up in another vast room. There was a woodwork shop where various items of furniture were being crafted. Some were basic, others had beautiful African designs. The church had their own bakery, they purified their own water, and had a vast generator which would kick in within thirty seconds of the national grid cutting out, ensuring a power supply to the whole complex. It was an incredible place, very African and unique.

Attached to one end of the auditorium was a large six-storey building with a few more floors above under construction. On top of this was a radio mast sending out radio broadcasts. In this building were offices, dormitories, a shop, and accommodation for the continual stream of visitors who came to the church.

As our bus pulled up, we had our first taste of one slightly unusual church tradition – the video camera. Everything that happened in the church seemed to be filmed, an African *Big Brother*! We were filmed getting off the bus and waiting to be taken to our rooms. For those like me, who hate seeing themselves on TV, it took some getting used to.

I sat there with my senses whirling. I recognised the smells, the sounds, and the humidity but everything else was very alien. I was glad to be taken to our dormitory and given a chance to rest as we had flown overnight on a crowded flight. We had two large dormitories for our group. They were basic but air conditioned and clean. Each had its own bathroom with a couple of showers, toilets and a sink. Having a shower curtain instead of a door on the toilet cubicle was a bit weird but not that difficult to live with. We also had use of a large dining room where meals were brought to us and where we watched teaching videos. We were regarded as guests of the church and well looked after.

The group I was with consisted mainly of members from Trine's church in Haywards Heath. It was a new church started by a South African who felt called to come to England. Many members of the church had been out to Lagos, including the pastor who came again on our trip. The trip had been organised by Fiona, a lady whose son lived permanently at the church in Lagos. There was a small group from a church in Tunbridge Wells, a couple from New Zealand and a pastor from America. It was a lovely group who made me feel very welcome.

We spent Saturday resting and exploring the church and preparing for the main service on Sunday. In the evening I went down into the main auditorium. The heat was intense, made worse by the layer of smelly insect repellent I had covered myself in. The place was full of people working away on the building and a choir having a practice in one corner. The set-up reminded me of how great cathedrals once operated. Even when under construction they were places where people met. At one time workmen could be building, a Mass taking place, and people coming and going about their business. It was just the same in the vast auditorium. People came to pray at the altar surrounded by rubble and noise. This vast piece of construction was still being built and hidden behind a vast wooden scaffold that in itself was a marvel. It used to be the practice for people to pray at the altar in the old building and now people prayed on the edge of what would be the new altar rail. It's not a practice that I would normally follow but it made a lot of sense to have an area to kneel and pray when so much activity went on around. I spent some time praying, on my knees until I couldn't bear it on the hard concrete, soft Westerner that I am, and cross-legged afterwards. Some people say they can't hear themselves think when surrounded by lots of noise. I find the opposite; as long as the noise is so great that you can't focus on one particular distraction, my brain is able to concentrate. I tried to humble myself before God, asking him to do what he wanted throughout the week. I just wanted to hear something from God and to be closer to him, even if I had to go home and continue living with the disease.

Others from the group had come down and were exploring. We sat sweating and chatting for a while. There was a real sense of anticipation amongst the group. We were all wondering what was going to happen in that vast room the next day and to us that week. Some of the group were obviously excited; others were quite nervous like me.

The church wanted us to see one of their services so we would know what typically took place before we were involved. We were up at 5.30am on the Sunday. This was the time that those wishing to be prayed for arrived at the gates. It was an amazing sight to see over a hundred people waiting before the sun had even risen. There was a process to be followed if you required prayer in the service and it was all very well ordered. First each person was interviewed to find out why they had come for prayer. People were then sorted. There was a section for people with AIDS, a section for people with cancer. A group of pregnant women were gathered together. Each person had an A3 piece of paper on which was written why they had come. Those with AIDS had to have a certificate from their hospital which all AIDS victims are given after they have been tested. They had to bring these for proof. Each case was documented and those healed would have to be retested and given an all-clear certificate from a hospital before they could testify that they had been healed.

We were ushered back to our rooms for breakfast. When we returned to the auditorium around 8.30am the place was filling up. We had an area to sit in with white plastic garden chairs and a few fans. It felt odd to have our own area but I learnt later that the congregation was divided up into cells who sat together. It made sense when in such a large congregation otherwise you would never get to know anyone. Our chairs and fans were a recognition that we were not used to the heat or sitting for hours on small wooden benches, all part of the hospitality shown to visitors. There was a choir who wore black trousers or skirts and white shirts. It included a group known as the disciples. These were people, some Westerners and some Africans, who lived in the church. They studied there and helped to run it. One of their tasks was to look after our group. They were on hand to take us from place to place and to help us understand what was going on.

We had to set aside Western concepts of what we thought a church service should be like. The service lasted from around 8am to 6pm. It involved worship led by the choir. They mainly sang Western songs which made it easy to join in. There was prayer. The congregation listened to preaching tapes played over the PA. There were loads of TV screens everywhere. You could see at least one from every spot in the church. Previously filmed testimonies were shown. There was no order of service that we could distinguish but always something going on. Some people seemed to come and stay all day, others came and went. There was a continual flow of human traffic. The construction work didn't stop either.

Suddenly into this came TB Joshua. He was called the Overseer of the church. He started the church eight years ago with eight members. Now there were around thirty thousand, although I doubt anybody knew the exact number. He was referred to as the anointed man of God and the Prophet because of the things God did through him. He was held in high regard by the whole congregation. It was harder for someone like me to identify with the respect shown to his position. He was a normal man, but one to whom you acted in a certain way. From hearing people speak about him I expected a fanfare and a state arrival. Instead he was suddenly there, walking around the church auditorium, then he was gone again. He didn't stay through all of the service but came and went a few times.

Then it was time for the sick to be prayed for. TB Joshua was there with a camera crew who filmed everything, which was relayed on many TV screens so that the congregation could see what was going on. The visitors were taken to the action by the disciples. It felt odd to be ushered around the church, to be the special guests. But that was how we were regarded in one sense, guests who would need to see things happen in front of them rather than watch them on a TV screen.

Those in the emergency section were prayed for first. The people in this group were clearly ill and in pain. They had various skin conditions which were very unpleasant. In places their skin was peeling off, weeping and sore. In some cases the skin was rotten away to the bone. I'm not sure if all the medical conditions described as cancer were what doctors in the West would call cancer but the church referred to obvious skin problems as cancer. These people were clearly ill and we accepted that the Africans regarded their serious skin problems as cancer.

TB Joshua went to the first guy in the line. He had skin cancer and his skin was peeling off his legs. TB Joshua dealt with him in an unexpected way, by our standards. He looked at the guy and told him to confess what he had been doing. The guy didn't respond at first so TB Joshua said he was a thief and needed to confess. The guy didn't answer and so he moved on to the next person in the line.

I need to set the scene a bit. The line of sick were on benches alongside the wall of an area attached to the main auditorium. TB Joshua had his aides around him and two camera crews which included guys with camera lights. The visitors lined up close by with the disciples who were explaining to us what was going on. A running commentary was being given over the PA in English, then repeated in French, followed by an African language. TB Joshua had a radio mike which he would tap when he wanted the commentary to stop so he could speak to the congregation, or for all to hear what he was saying to the person. It was, at times, difficult to understand both TB Joshua's accent and that of the people he spoke to so the disciples translated the African English into Western English, whispering in our ears, telling us what was being said. So while TB Joshua was talking to the guy with skin cancer I was hearing over the PA; 'The man has skin cancer. The man is a thief, a thief, he must confess. He will not confess.' At the same time a disciple was whispering in my ear. It was weird and very different to how healing services would be conducted in England.

As the first guy didn't seem to want to confess anything TB Joshua had moved on to the next person in the line. Suddenly the first guy indicated that he wanted to say something. TB Joshua, camera crew and entourage returned to him. He admitted he was a thief but TB Joshua asked him; 'What do you do?' It seemed odd when the guy had just said he was a thief but he insisted; 'What do you do?' He wouldn't answer so again the entourage moved on. Again he indicated he was ready to open up. After an exchange between the two, which was hard to follow as the background commentary blared out, the guy confessed. He was in a gang which went into people's houses, killed everybody there and then stole everything. The guy was both a thief and a murderer. Finally TB Joshua was willing to pray for him. I didn't see his skin heal instantly before my eyes but he walked away, no longer looking in pain.

As TB Joshua moved down the line it seemed that for each person needing prayer there was a situation, not always directly related to the illness, that he drew to their attention and that needed dealing with. For one man it was a situation with his wife whom it seemed had stolen from him and didn't respect him. He challenged the parents of a young boy with kidney failure who had taken him to a witch doctor. He told people that they had to confess certain sins before he would pray for them. He was quite firm with many. To others he showed more compassion. He told one guy whose parents were both witch doctors, who could possibly kill him for coming to see TB Joshua, that he was safe in the church. So often the illness seemed secondary. What was clear was that TB Joshua was telling people things about their lives that had not been fed to him. He was receiving words from God to challenge individuals.

What I understood from what was going on in front of me was that TB Joshua took sin far more seriously than sickness. He was more concerned with challenging people about their actions than asking God to heal their sickness. Why? Because their sickness could only kill their body, their sin could kill their soul. In Africa people are more open to spiritual things. They believe in witch doctors, spiritual forces and demon possession. Sick people are willing to try anything to be healed. They will try the medical doctor and if he can't help, or they can't afford any more treatment, they may try a witch doctor. These witch doctors' ceremonies involve some horrid, horrid practices. When people hear of someone healing people by the hundred they are happy to give it a try. They do not necessarily accept the Christian faith.

It's easy to judge these people from our comfortable Western position. It's easier to understand their desperation and willingness to go wherever when you see cancer eating through their skin. They have no money for chemotherapy and radiotherapy, they dare not risk amputating the affected area. They are truly desperate and in continual pain. However, they find something else when they come to this church. They may expect a quick prayer and then a complete healing but what they get is a challenge to turn from sin, the gospel told plainly, and a call to change their whole lives. It was the fact that the guy was a thief and murderer that needed dealing with, more than the cancer that was eating him alive.

Did TB Joshua teach that sin causes sickness? He certainly did to the AIDS patient who was living a life of promiscuity. To those who confessed sins and were healed he said that their healing was not guaranteed. If they continued to sin they could fall ill again. I didn't hear him preach on it but the church seem to believe that the sin of an adult could affect a child, and future generations to come. Yet in many of the cases I saw, both in the services and on the video testimonies, sin wasn't mentioned at all. On one video, I saw a guy who had been shot in the leg and could no longer walk. TB Joshua prayed for him and he walked. The video showed him driving away in a car. The guy didn't confess a sin. In the majority of cases, TB Joshua just prayed for people. I think he linked sin to sickness where he believed it was the cause, but where it wasn't he prayed and people were healed. What was clear was that he encouraged people to confess their sins and ask God for forgiveness. Once this was done the sin was dealt with. There was no sin so great that it couldn't be forgiven. Any curses placed on people by witch doctors could be broken. Any consequences of sin passed from parent to child could finish there and then. This guy believed that Jesus had defeated sin and all its consequences, including sickness.

After praying for those in the emergency section he prayed for the AIDS section. To be honest I can't remember what happened on the Sunday when he prayed for this group so I'll describe what happened on the Wednesday service. He moved his arm one direction and the whole group swayed and staggered in that direction, then he moved his arm the other way and they went with it. Then he blew loudly down his mike and they all fell over. That was that.

Yes, it was weird and no, I didn't understand it. The way he prayed for people was vastly different from what I had ever seen before. He rarely touched people. Sometimes he touched the corresponding part of his body to the part of the sick person. An obvious example was when he prayed for a woman with breast cancer. He put his hand on his own breast as he prayed. The laying on of hands is instructed in the Bible but whether he didn't touch the lady out a sense of propriety, I don't know. He seemed to lay hands directly on the men more often. People did react physically as he prayed. They fell over or swayed and at times he moved people by directing his hands and they slumped and staggered in whatever direction he pointed. The most difficult thing to accept was that many people he prayed for promptly vomited. It was explained to me that they were throwing up the illness within them.

After the AIDS victims, he worked his way round a large circle with over a hundred people in line for various illnesses. You could read what the request for prayer was from what was written on their placard. They ranged from asthma to infertility. There was a child there whose placard had the words 'disobedient spirit' written on it. It would be interesting to see what a child psychologist would make of that.

There was a group of men whom he seemed to be instructing to kneel but they wouldn't. A disciple whispered in my ear that some of the men were too proud to bow before God and so would not be prayed for. Some didn't seem to respond at all. While some people were emotional, crying out and weeping, others looked like blocks of stone refusing to show any sign that anything was happening in or around them. I was told that Nigerians in particular don't like to show emotion, it's seen as a sign of weakness. It was odd seeing people give testimonies of being healed but showing no joy at all. I don't think it was wrong, rather culturally conditioned.

TB Joshua prayed for some pregnant women who were all overdue. Unless you have lots of money, and not always then, you don't risk a caesarean in Lagos. He prayed for each and told them to go and have their babies. For some he told them what the sex of the baby would be and what to call it. Apparently, although it didn't happen on this occasion, it's common for a woman to go into labour there and then. They have a maternity room and a midwife on hand in the church and the women sometimes go and give birth naturally. At one part of the service they gave thanks for the new-born babies. The mothers danced around with their babies. Some of our group were given babies to cuddle and encouraged to dance around with them. Someone tried to drag me in front of a camera and I was told to dance. I have my own cultural idiosyncrasies which don't include dancing for cameras so I refused.

Nobody was asked to pay anything to the church. The church members gave a tithe and supported the work of the church. Everybody who was prayed for was given a free meal. TB Joshua taught that you should care for your body and eat properly. The church gave money to the sick who had spent everything seeking medical aid so that they could eat healthily and regain their strength.

Testimony was encouraged. People came back for special testimony meetings which went on throughout the week. These were videoed. I did not see those who were prayed for while I was there return and give their testimonies. What I saw, both live and on various videos, were cases of people prayed for in other services. In many ways the videos were better because they showed the person's condition before and after. They showed cases of horrid skin cancer being prayed for and then the person coming back showing the area healed. You could see scars but could not deny they were well. AIDS victims came back with their all-clear certificates. The church seemed very keen to show the healings in context, the original condition and the present condition.

Could it be fake? Yes, I could have been deceived. The skin conditions could have been created with make-up and the testimonies given by actors. If it was all one enormous lie then it was a very good one, well executed and on a mass scale that would rival the filming of a Disney blockbuster. I am not exaggerating numbers; hundreds were claiming healings. That's a lot of actors and a lot of organisation. If it was fake I have to ask why, for what purpose? Nobody appeared to be getting rich. Yes, TB Joshua had a flat in the building and wore a suit but if I was him I wouldn't be living in that part of Lagos, surrounded by the noise of the building work and the continual presence of so many people. But more importantly, if I were God, would I be allowing so much deceit done in my name? TB Joshua continually said that it was Jesus not he who healed. He had no power; it was Jesus working through him by the Holy Spirit. I saw what I saw. If it wasn't of God, then I have been truly deceived and God's name severely misused.

12. I Will Open up my Heart and Let the Healer Set me Free[1]

We spent most of Monday watching videos of teaching sessions taken by TB Joshua. I didn't find the teaching particularly stimulating. The videos were hard to follow as he had a strong African accent. Realising that his audience did not always understand him he would write sentences up on a blackboard. At times he would say a sentence, write it, repeat it, rub it out and start on his next one. It could be painfully slow going. I found the teaching quite simplistic in one sense and felt he didn't answer the questions put to him by his audience. It felt rather rude not to appreciate watching these videos but try as I might, I couldn't persuade myself that I was learning anything vital.

On Tuesday the talk amongst the group turned to confessions. The church believed that it was right to confess sin to one another and sometimes publicly. I had heard it said that sin only exits the body through the mouth. It's in confessing that sin is dealt with. Knowing that we could be asked to give a confession, some of our group began to write down what they wished to confess. Various approaches were taken. Some prayed and wrote down one or two things. Others took a blanket approach and wrote mini novels. One guy, whom I had made friends with, and I don't think will mind me saying this, was so concerned about doing this confession in front of other members in the group that he asked if I'd listen to a practice read-through. I offered marks on diction, general presentation and I felt the work flowed well. Sorry, I jest, it was a serious issue and a big hurdle for all of us.

I didn't get it. I couldn't work out why we needed to do this, and certainly didn't see why it had to be public. We were told that we would receive some teaching on confession before we had to confess. I was content to wait and hear what was said before I made my decision. It wasn't that I didn't think I had anything to confess or that confession wasn't a necessary part of a healthy Christian lifestyle. In fact it was almost the opposite. As I have already written, since having cancer I had done quite a lot of confessing with Andy. My problem lay in the fact that I believed once something was confessed you accepted Jesus' forgiveness and it was in the past, and forgotten by God. I wasn't happy with the idea that you had to regurgitate it. If my sins were removed as far from me as the east was from the west, then I wasn't in the mood to go travelling to find them. Of course I wasn't any more comfortable thinking about confessing in front of anyone in our group. Like everyone else, I found the thought of it being taped very sobering. However, I debated, was I willing to do whatever it would take to be healed? But the feeling that there were hoops to jump through before I could be healed concerned me. It wasn't tying up with my understanding of how God worked. It was that image of God with the stick again. I couldn't picture him up in his heaven saying that unless John does this, this and this, I'm not healing him. Yet, in contrast to these thoughts, I couldn't help but wonder, what if I do have to do this and it's one of those things that you see the value of once done?

We didn't get our teaching on confession. As Tuesday afternoon began the disciples came and set up a similar version of what we had seen early on Sunday morning. We were to be interviewed and a placard written with the reason we had come for prayer. We would be interviewed on camera. Then we would go and do our confession. None of this was compulsory; each individual stage was optional. But I felt my arm was being twisted. I had to do this if I was to be healed. I need to be clear here. My arm was not twisted by the disciples or anyone in my group. The side of me that worries that I'm not doing it right, twisted my arm, if you can twist your own!

I considered the whole process as another of the horrible things that I had to go through to reach the end result. Just as I had to lose my inhibitions and be naked in front of people, have things shoved up me, have dreadful treatment which made me ill, all to try and beat cancer, I felt I had to do the filmed interviews and confession. The cooler, rational side of my brain shut down. Nobody forced me to do anything but I got more and more wound up.

I started the process. I had an embarrassing discussion with three African ladies who didn't understand what bowel cancer was. It was excruciating trying to explain. I think they were more used to external sicknesses when referring to cancer. They struggled with what couldn't be seen and had no obvious symptoms. I tried to explain that I had cancer, I had finished treatment. My original symptoms were now gone but I still had cancer. They jumped on the original symptom of bleeding. They wrote down 'Rectal bleeding' and sent me off to the next person saying I would be prayed for and the bleeding would stop. But the bleeding had stopped after my September operation. The side effects of my treatment were gone and I was feeling fine. This didn't mean I was in the clear in any way. Thankfully the lady who wrote my banner understood what bowel cancer was but the damage was done. I now wasn't only wound up, I was angry and hurting.

Next was the video interview, a repeat of my first attempt to explain what was wrong, made even worse by the camera. I dug my heels in when they asked me about symptoms and said as clearly as possible, but through clenched teeth, that I had bowel cancer. It was a serious condition, I needed a major operation and my chances of survival were slim. I doubt you will be seeing that on any of the videos they distribute.

Come confession time, I was on the verge of all-out rage. I expected a separate room with a guy, maybe two, who would hear my confession. What I got was a table in the middle of the room within earshot of everyone and three Western girls, all quite a lot younger than me. They didn't seem to follow all the little gender rules we have; men talking to men, women to women. They also didn't see confession as a private one-on-one deal. They certainly didn't make it easy. I flipped and out came all the questions I wanted answered before they were getting so much as a minor sin out of me. My frustrated questions were met by kind answers. They didn't get wound up by me asking questions, nor respond to my mood. They answered each question calmly and finished by saying that I was clearly not ready to give a confession. I didn't have to if I didn't want to. I should go away and think about what I wanted to do. I was taken aback somewhat but still wound up.

It only took one kind word from someone in the group to push me over the edge. I lost the tight control I was holding and ran for it. I think the door may have slammed behind me but it wasn't a deliberate slam in anger. I didn't storm off; I just couldn't cope with the whole thing. Everything hurt. I was confused and more than anything I wanted to go home. If an airline rep had met me on the stairs at that point and offered an instant flight home I would have taken it, without a shadow of doubt, and paid any price for the ticket. After some consideration I had decided not to ask anybody to come with me for company. At that point I wished someone had come just to be there for no other reason than to look after me. I took refuge on my bed and cried. I had regained my control by the time one of the guys came down to the dorm. I talked about how I was feeling. I told him how I confessed everything that I thought needed dealing with before I came to Lagos and how I felt I was only going through the whole process because I had to. He simply said that maybe I didn't need to do a confession but that I should pray about it and see if God led me to anything in particular.

I was called back upstairs by the disciples who wanted to know if I was ready to confess. Again out came the questions and the tears and again it was met with calm indifference. They were not going to be drawn into responding to my emotions. They said to call for them when I was ready. I went back to my dorm.

I decided eventually that in the grand scheme of things, in the light of this wretched operation that seemed to be looming, I would not take any chances. I'd try the blanket approach and write down a few things, okay, a few pages, of anything I felt needed confessing. I sent a message saying I would do it, I'd carpet bomb the whole issue and that would be that. They said they would come and get me when it was time but they never did. I never gave that confession.

Things happen on a very different time frame in Lagos. Around 10pm we were told we would receive a lecture from TB Joshua. We got ourselves ready with Bibles, notepads and pens. Some of our group had to be woken and got out of bed! In true British style we were ready and waiting fifteen minutes after the call. There we waited for over half an hour, maybe more. In came TB

Joshua, finally up close and personal. He was quite normal, wearing Western clothes, welcoming us all. He said that one of his disciples was to lecture us. Some in our group were disappointed but to be honest I was relieved. There was no way I would have been able to stay awake if I had to struggle to understand his accent and watch him write on the board. Fiona's son gave us the lecture.

I have never heard a person of that age speak so well. He could only have been in his early twenties but he had me in the palm of his hand from the first word. He was eloquent and clear. He quoted scripture after scripture, it was like water flowing through what he said. His title was 'The Good Life'. He started by saying that many Christians wonder why their lives were not full of the power of God and the peace of God. They wondered why they weren't living the good Christian life. He said that the answer lay within us. Jesus had done his part, he had died for us. He said that the Holy Spirit came after Jesus as comforter and guide and wished to dwell within us. It was sin that stopped the Holy Spirit from fully dwelling within us and being able to work with and through us. He said that the key thing we had to deal with was sin. We needed to repent, but that true repentance involved changing the way we lived.

I'm not a great fan of sermons. I find many a bit on the dull side, but this guy had me hanging on every word. Things began to slot into place. As he was speaking he used a phrase that drove into my brain. He said that Christians should be people who pursue righteousness. As he said this something in my head answered back; 'You don't do that.' I realised that I did not pursue righteousness. I did not passionately pursue doing the right thing, and I did not hunger after righteousness. From that point on as he spoke it felt like every other thing he said was 'pursue righteousness'.

I went to bed and didn't sleep a wink to about 5am. God had pinpointed the thing that I needed to confess, the thing that I had done wrong for so long and didn't even realise that it needed dealing with. I didn't take sin seriously and I didn't pursue a righteous life. I knew that was what I had to confess. The disciples never came and asked me to make my confession. I was not told, as some of our group were, that I needed to confess in the main meeting. Yet my confession was now so central to what I learnt in Lagos that it had to be told as part of the whole story.

If you had asked me before I went to Lagos, was I a sinner, I would have said 'Yes'. This answer would be based on my belief that I was born a sinner, being part of a sinful world. It would have also been based on the obvious fact that I knew I sinned. If you had asked me was I a big sinner, had I committed any of the big ones, then I would have said 'no'. I've not murdered anybody, not committed adultery. I treated others properly and did my best to be an all round nice kind of bloke. I struggled to find any big sins to confess because, if I'm really honest, I think I'm pretty good. Yes, I slipped up now and then but would ask Jesus to forgive me. All in all, I was okay.

As I lay in my bed that night it wasn't the big sins that kept coming to mind, it was the little ones. I literally found myself examining attitude after attitude. I'll give some examples, quickly, before I chicken out. Did I think gossip was wrong? Ultimately, yes. Did that stop me doing it? No. Why? Because I didn't actually think it was that important. Speeding, nobody likes this one. Is it legal to speed? No. Is this a law that we don't have to keep? Of course not. What was my attitude to it? I couldn't care less that every day I broke the speed limit, not accidentally but deliberately. To my shame I recalled that only a few weeks earlier I had been driving the hire car in

France, bringing a group of staff to the campsite. The issue of speeding had come up and a debate was taking place as to whether we really had to keep the limits. I actually smirked to myself, amused that none of them had noticed, or were willing to comment, that I was doing double the speed limit for the road I was on. Oh, sinful wretched man that I am. It wasn't the individual sins that God was convicting me about, it was my attitude. I couldn't care less if I sinned. I either justified my actions, saying the most basic things which were wrong were in fact not wrong, or I would say I couldn't help it. I wasn't even trying to do the right thing in so many areas.

I know that there are many grey areas where we have to make a judgement call as to whether something is right or wrong. We have a conscience, God given, to help us. I'm saying I was making all my own judgement calls over whether something was right or wrong for many small matters where it is quite clear what the answer was.

Part of the challenge lay in my character. People may be different but when I really looked hard I couldn't put a finger on a time when I truly had been so tempted to do wrong that I actually couldn't stop myself. It wasn't that I was never tempted to do the wrong thing, it's just I can't honestly say that I had no choice. When I did wrong, I chose to do so. I'd never been so influenced by someone or something that the choice had been taken from me. I'd become quite adept at dealing with my conscience. I could fool it into thinking what I was doing wrong was, in fact, quite okay. I justified my way around it. Speeding, everybody does it, it's not that important. Those cameras are there to make money, wish someone would go around putting plastic bags over the lenses. It's an invasion of my civil liberties. See the thought pattern? If that didn't ease my conscience, I'd try another approach. I'd ignore it.

Who cares? Jesus will forgive me. Civil liberties! Tell that to the parents of the child you've just mown down!

Christians should pursue righteousness. What a joke! Not only was I not trying, I didn't even feel I needed to bother. What's more, I even had the barefaced cheek to blame God. Why was he not removing the temptation, and why was he not rewarding my efforts when I did do the right thing? I'd even gone down the line of saying that as I'd not been rewarded for being a good little Christian boy with the things I'd asked God for, then I was jolly well going to have a bit of a rebellion. I'd show that God, he'd have to forgive me anyway.

I was the most foolish of creatures. Who was I to set my own rules, to think I could negotiate, even blatantly to think I could use the gift of forgiveness as a tool when I couldn't work my way around the thing I wanted to do? I wouldn't want to go through that night again. Thing after thing, that I had no longer even bothered to regard as sin and ask for forgiveness for, kept coming to my mind. I woke knowing without a shadow of doubt what my confession was. I didn't take sin seriously and it was time to.

The guy concluded his teaching by saying that it is sin in our lives that stops the Holy Spirit working to his maximum potential. The good life is not one without struggles but as you open yourself to the Holy Spirit, he is able to guide you, work through you and you can find God's power and his peace in all situations. But sin that isn't dealt with will block all that. I do not believe this negates what I have said in previous chapters about the value of Christ's death or the amazing reality of grace. Forgiveness can only be found through what Jesus did for us on the cross. Sin's curse is broken. I can still choose to sin; I still have free will. The path that God wants us to take is one away from sin. We will fight it all our lives but we can win. We can, and should, pursue righteousness.

I didn't need to go to Lagos for the healer to set me free from cancer. I needed to go for God to show me a far more dangerous cancer that I had allowed to grow. He showed me I could be healed from this cancer of sin but I had to choose to and strive to live in that healing.

In Lagos after people confessed publicly, they often said; 'I will go and sin no more.' They weren't being foolish believing they would never sin again. They were saying that they would strive to sin no more. Have I found it easy not to sin? No. My car, used to higher speeds, objects to any thirty mile an hour limit. Am I better off for trying? Most definitely.

> Love incarnate, love divine
> Captivate this heart of mine
> Till all I do speaks of you.[2]

Notes

1   Martin Smith, *Over The Mountains And The Sea* (© 1994 Curious? Music/admin by Bucks Music Group Ltd)
2   Stuart Townend, *Love Incarnate* (© 2002 Thankyou Music)

13. Hear my Cry, O God; Listen to my Prayer

(Psalm 61:1)

What of cancer, the equally real physical one? Wednesday was the big day. The Western visitors would join the prayer line and what would happen? The sense of anticipation built throughout the day. During the Sunday service TB Joshua had said that he had words for the visitors, their time would come. Before we knew it, it was upon us.

We had been in the service for a few hours during the afternoon. Africa can be all hurry hurry wait wait. We had suddenly been rushed down into the auditorium as if we were about to miss something important. For two hours nothing happened except a teaching tape was played over the PA. It was a poor-quality recording, you couldn't make out a word. Then we were ushered up to the dining room for tea. The food we had in Lagos was basic but okay. Tea was the meal which had the tendency to be a bit odd. One day it was soup, another just a doughnut. On Wednesday it was rather stodgy pancakes. We had to raid the boxes of leftover goodies that the Westerners bring and leave, if unused, for the next group for some suitable pancake fillings. Then it was all hurry hurry you must get in the prayer line. As I took my place I was regretting eating a single pancake.

We were all put in the main prayer line, a large circle of over one hundred people. Our plastic white chairs awaited us with our placards. First the junior prophets

went round the circle praying for people. These were
guys training under TB Joshua. Various helpers stood
behind the people as they were prayed for, holding up
their placards. As they moved round the circle towards us
things began to happen. People shook, fell over, others
threw up. When they got to me I had to close my eyes as I
couldn't cope with the cameras in my face. Behind me I
heard the commentator, 'Look on your TV screens, you
will see the man from England, he has cancer.' I didn't fall
over, in fact I only knew they had moved on because the
camera lights were no longer burning through my
eyelids.

At some point while they prayed, TB Joshua arrived.
Apparently he walked around looking at all of us,
including me. I didn't notice as I had my eyes shut. TB
Joshua began to pray for people one by one. I'd love to
tell you how he dealt with each person, what he said,
how he challenged and how he prayed. But those are the
stories for the individuals to tell. All I can say was that it
was both powerful and scary. He had some challenging
words to say to people: things which were at times
deeply private and at times deeply painful. People
responded in various ways. Some fell over, some
vomited, some shook, others were calm. It was a powerful time.

He got to the person on my right and prayed with
them. He then passed me by and spoke to the person on
my left, taking no notice of me at all. He moved on down
the line and then returned for a second time. Again he
spoke to the person on my right and moved directly on to
the person on my left. This time he wanted to pray for
her. I was sitting on the corner of the circle. There was one
of those horrible moments when I knew I was in the way
but didn't know what to do. He motioned for me to move
forward and leave space around the person he was

praying for. I stepped forward, trying to avoid the many cables that trailed from the cameras and lights. These had already proved lethal when the camera crew had rushed from one place to another. The wires had caught round our ankles and literally pulled one of our group down. When I think of all the health and safety rules we have at Spring Harvest, how every wire must be taped down firmly, you can but laugh at wires draped all over the place and not a hint of yellow and black striped gaffer tape in sight.

He prayed for the person next to me and moved on. I didn't quite know what to do, whether to return to my seat or stay where I had been put. As he reached the end of the line he turned and said that he would see everybody individually.

After he had finished his second round of praying for the Westerners, the disciples had been taking people away to talk to them. I found myself alone sitting among a line of empty white chairs. My placard was thrust into my hand. It was over. I didn't feel disappointed. Having witnessed what had happened to various members of our group, I felt extremely relieved and wasn't sure I wanted the guy to come anywhere near me at all. I was also confused. I was the only person in the group with a life-threatening illness. I was the only person he didn't pray for.

Fiona, our group organiser, came over. She was direct. She told me not to be upset that he didn't pray for me, there was a reason. She felt that he had moved me to one side for a reason. Others in our group said later that they thought he moved me in the Spirit, that I didn't voluntarily move. They attributed this to my awkward steps. I assured them that he moved me because I was in the way and that I knew what I was doing. I moved awkwardly because I was in danger of losing my balance to the camera wires. Fiona reminded me of the fact that TB Joshua knew I was coming. If you have a serious condition, you have to ask if you can go. They pray about it and decide if they will issue an invite. He had invited me. Fiona said that she had felt that someone with a serious illness was going to come on the trip and she had not been surprised when at the last moment I joined. She reminded me of what he had said when he left the circle; he would see me individually. Maybe what he had to say was not to be said in front of the thousands of church members who were now sitting watching the Westerners on the TV.

I decided I wasn't going to be disappointed. I wouldn't go and hide. I would stay to the end of the service. I did go and get a drink and stood watching one of the outside TVs as our group were interviewed. I never quite got to the bottom of how they decided who would give a public confession and even to this day I wonder why they had to do it, but they did. I was amazed at the bravery of these people confessing to sins that you would never want spoken of in public. I still don't agree with the church's definition of what it means to confess sins to one another and I find the confession tapes they sell sickening. Those guys were amazingly brave. I don't think I could have done it. They also gave testimony to what had happened to them. This didn't seem in line with the church's practice of people returning at a later date to give testimony. Maybe it was different for Westerners who would be returning home shortly. All I can say is that my time in Lagos raised almost as many questions as those which were answered. My 'i's were not all dotted, nor my 't's crossed.

* * *

I was able to join in the rest of the service. It wasn't until the following day that I felt disappointed. At breakfast everyone was talking about the night before. The tension that had built up throughout the whole trip had peaked. People had come, joined the line and been prayed for. What was going to happen, had now happened. But not for me. The other topic of conversation was why hadn't he prayed for John?

When the time came to watch more teaching videos I couldn't stand it and took refuge in my dorm. I didn't want to watch another video. When we were called to go to see some testimonies, I didn't go. I was sick of them. I didn't want to see another video, listen to another testimony. I wanted to go home. I felt bitterly disappointed. Why had he not prayed for me? Why did I have to come to Lagos? Why, when God seemed to be pouring out his blessing and speaking so directly, did he have nothing to say to me?

Fiona came to find me and as is so often the way with me, a kind word turned anger into tears. I felt wretched and longed to escape the place. She asked two of the disciples to come and speak with me. They were incredibly kind. They told me that TB Joshua would see me, it was guaranteed and to trust that God had a plan. Again they were very professional, very calm.

Again the gender rules were bent, a girl and a guy came to see me. Maybe the guy was a concession to the fact we were in the male dorm sitting on my bed. He seemed genuinely concerned for me and how I was feeling. What they said helped. I asked some questions about what my meeting with TB would be like; mainly would there be cameras? I was told they would be there but I could ask for them to go away for a moment. They also had practical advice too. I could sit and hide away from the group all day stewing or I could go back and join the others and wait and see what would happen. I did so. The talk had helped shift the disappointment.

I think Thursday was the worst day. It dragged and nothing seemed to happen. We watched video after video. We had been going up onto the top floors which were still under construction. There, if you found the right spot, you could catch a breeze and enjoy being outdoors. Air conditioning is great but not pleasant on a permanent basis. You could also enjoy a few moments on your own. Unfortunately our little hideaways were discovered and we were told we could not go on the roof. They weren't being mean. They were generally concerned we might hurt ourselves, or worse, fall out of one of the glassless windows. We felt like caged animals. By the afternoon some of us guys were having pillow fights, trying to get rid of some of our pent-up energy. We succeeded in breaking a bed but not releasing the tension.

In comparison Friday was all activity. It was our last day. We were leaving at 7am Saturday morning but would be spending the night in an all-night prayer meeting. During the afternoon we were given three lectures, back to back, from the disciples. They were good, again the eloquence and the passion of these young guys was truly amazing. But my mind was now focused on seeing TB Joshua. Would anything happen? Would he pray for me? Would I receive a complete healing from cancer? If not, would he say something that would help me through what lay ahead? The tension kept on mounting.

During the late afternoon we were taken to Prayer Mountain. Throughout the week Fiona had been trying to persuade the disciples to take us. I have no idea why they chose that particular moment. Prayer Mountain is in fact a swamp in the middle of the city. It was the site of the original church. They bought the land cheaply as it couldn't be used for buildings. What they had done with it is as equally impressive as the giant church building. They had cleared the swamp into some lovely lakes and waterways. Around these, on little islands or on stilts, were thatched prayer huts. Some were linked with walkways, others you had to get to by boat. Some had rooms, including bedrooms. Others were simple open-sided thatched huts. The idea was that visitors and church members could ask to go there to pray. It was an oasis of calm, much needed in the busy and dirty city of Lagos.

Our tour would have been idyllic if it hadn't been for the incredibly heavy storm overhead. The rain beat down for the whole time we were there. The heavy clouds made it very dark and there was a lot of lightning and crashing thunder. Under white umbrellas we had a tour of the walkways and then were packed off in boats for a paddle around. It was all fun, despite the rain, and went some way to ease the growing tension I felt.

It was dark by the time we returned. The all-night prayer meeting was cancelled as people couldn't get there because of the rain. The city's power was out leaving the great church generator to provide the power needed to light the compound and run the air-conditioning units. We were told to pack and rest. TB would see us soon.

Around 10pm we were ushered upstairs. The dining room chairs had been put in two rows. We were placed in the order we would see TB. I noticed that I was only a few people from the end. Even now, no privileges. It was another rush rush wait wait time. He began to see us at midnight. It was my turn at 1.30am. They just don't keep to the same time pattern we do.

Suddenly the moment was upon me, I was sitting opposite TB Joshua. As I sat down he turned and started talking to one of his disciples. Imagine you are to see the Queen. For days you know this is going to happen. For hours you have waited, wondering when the final moment will come. Suddenly there you are, face to face, and she turns and starts a chat with her lady-in-waiting. You don't know where to look or if you should be hearing the conversation.

The room was full of disciples standing round the edge with a central table and a chair each side. On one side sat TB Joshua with the TV crew behind him, the other side was my chair. It was all rather quiet. Suddenly he turned to me, put a mike to my mouth and asked me what I thought of TB Joshua. I looked at him with a dumb, dazed look, not knowing what to say. Yet another video for the bin, I fear. I'd never been asked to comment on a teacher by the teacher, face to face and while being filmed. I mumbled something about pursuing righteousness, not exactly along the flowing lines of the previous chapter. He muttered good good, and held out his hand, the signal he would pray for me. I foolishly didn't listen to a word he prayed, too busy wondering if I was actually awake and this was happening. He finished, gave me a bookmark with a text on it, and a small card with another Bible verse and went quiet. It was all over, time up.

That just couldn't be it. I couldn't have come all this way, been through all that had happened that week, for nothing, not a word. In desperation I asked him, 'Do you have anything for me?' Without pause he began to speak.

What he said isn't for this book. Some of it made sense, some I still have to work out. He didn't look at me as he spoke but around the room. To be honest, it felt as if he wasn't really that interested in talking to me at all. However, as he spoke he described aspects of my character and I knew he was talking about me. Some of the descriptions of me others would know about. A few things he said only I knew described me, my attitudes and responses to certain things. Not even my closest friends could have fed this to him. The guy was hearing from God.

None of what he said referred to cancer, although some things made it clear that a future lay ahead for me. He didn't mention the word cancer once. He finished and went quiet. Again in desperation I asked him the only question I really wanted the answer for: 'What about cancer?' His reply was brief and finished the conversation.

'It's finished, don't look back.'

* * *

I left that room with two conflicting emotions fighting to take the lead. An excitement was building. He had said it was finished. Was cancer really over? A negative thought also battled, he hadn't seemed interested in me. He spoke to me without any passion or interest. It was as if he just wanted to get me out the door so he could get to bed. Had he really heard from God or had he given me a glib answer?

Fiona had advised that we write down what he said to us before speaking to anybody. By the time I had finished writing everyone had headed down to the dorms. Being nearly the last, most people had had a good chat about it all and were now attempting to catch a few winks before the long flight home.

I looked over what he had said and cried. The tension broke and the tears flowed. Again, I was thrown into confusion. What on earth had just happened, what was it about? He must have been hearing from God because what he said was so personally about me. Yet he didn't seem interested in me at all.

Fiona found me and I told her what he had said. I told her why I was confused. She said that he wasn't interested in emotions, his role was purely to pass on what God had said to him. He didn't look at me because the way he heard from God and knew what to say was by reading words he saw around the room in the air. She said she'd get one of the disciples.

I think this time the disciples had had enough of being called to see me. It was getting late! But the disciple did ask me what had happened. She didn't comment on TB's attitude to me. She simply asked had I seen miracles while I was at the church. I had to answer yes. I had seen people healed. I remembered a guy I had seen in the prayer line on Wednesday. He had hobbled in with his knees all bandaged and danced out healed. She asked me if I thought TB Joshua heard from God. Again I had to say 'Yes.' I had heard the words he had given to people in our group. In later conversations they had admitted what he said was spot on, things which no one could have told him. I also had the evidence of what he had said about me. The guy was hearing from God. She said that I now had to choose: was what TB Joshua said about my cancer a word from God or not? I had to base my decision on what I had seen while at the church.

I allowed myself to begin to accept what he said: my cancer was over. I still had questions. One of guys in the group came and found me and we talked through what had happened. I wanted to know why TB Joshua had not prayed for me in the Wednesday meeting. He suggested that maybe he didn't need to, that at that point I did not have cancer which needed healing. He reminded me of the fact that TB Joshua had said he only prayed for the sick if he felt God telling him to. There had been times when he had not felt God tell him to pray and so he hadn't. When they say that everyone TB Joshua prays for is healed you need to add a little postscript. He doesn't pray for everyone, only those God instructs him to pray for. He didn't just ignore me; there was a reason.

The penny still hadn't dropped. I asked why the only thing he said the whole time I was there, about the very issue I had gone there for, why had it been so short, it's finished, don't look back. My friend asked a question in response. What did I most want to know about my cancer? What was the thing I most desperately sought? It was an end. I wanted it all to be over. If TB Joshua was truly speaking from God, what God had said was what I most wanted to hear, it was over. The doctors couldn't say it, but God could.

* * *

Never have I been so happy to return to England. My trip to Lagos was powerful but I'm not sure if I ever want to go there again. The intensity of the place and what had happened had left me exhausted. But I don't think I will ever be the same again.

* * *

I've had time to think through the significance of that week. I can now clearly see the value of the lessons God wished to teach me. I went to Lagos to learn to take sin seriously and this was as important for me to hear as what God had to say about my cancer.

Why didn't TB Joshua pray for me? When I went to Lagos there was no cancer in my body. He didn't pray for my healing from cancer because he didn't need to. It had been dealt with. Why then did I need to go all the way to Lagos for one man to pray for me? Why did I have to go anywhere to be healed? I didn't. I didn't need to go anywhere in particular, there was not one way I had to go to be healed. I think there is a value in why he didn't pray for me. God didn't want my healing to be attributed to the prayer of one man. He wanted to answer the prayers of the thousands who prayed for me. He could have answered the one prayer, but I think he wanted the thousands of prayers each to be answered.

In many ways the fact he didn't pray for me, in fact took very little notice of me at all, is a validation that this guy isn't out for glory or money. He could have made a dramatic testimonial video out of me, the young guy told he only had a 20% chance of surviving cancer, prayed for and healed by the anointed man of God, the man in the temple, Prophet TB Joshua! Instead I think he showed spiritual maturity and obeyed God.

Did treatment play a part? I think so. Medically speaking it is possible that the radiotherapy and chemotherapy did the trick. Does this mean prayer wasn't involved? I don't think so at all. We prayed asking God to get rid of the cancer, through treatment, through a miracle, any way, just do it. He did. The prayer I prayed each day while being zapped by lasers was answered.

Did confession play a part? Yes. Through the period from my diagnosis to my trip to Lagos, God dealt with many issues in my life, broke some powerful strongholds, convicted me of wrong attitudes and brought me to a much great understanding of my salvation.

Why do the words 'It's finished' mean so much? With cancer you never really get an all clear, there is always the chance it will return. In my case, it is more than just a chance. The percentages are stacked against me. The doctors still expect the cancer to come back. While it is thought that if it doesn't return within five years I should be clear, I have been told that this may not apply to me as my case is unusual. Medically there will never be an 'all clear.' Spiritually I believe I have been given a great gift, an all clear from the Manufacturer.

'Don't look back.' I don't think this means I should move on with my life without considering what has happened to me. I think this means don't look back expecting the cancer to return. I could live my life always looking back over my shoulder, the shadow of cancer always there, always wondering if the next scan would show something. I now don't have to live like that.

Can I prove any of this medically? No. The results of my first PET scan were inconclusive. There was no clearly visible active cancer. However, there was a swollen lymph gland that could contain active cancer cells. At the site of the original tumour in the bowel, scar tissue could be seen but the only way to tell if cancer cells were active within it would be to remove the bowel. The specialist that I had seen at St Mark's had suggested I have the surgery, regardless of the presence of any active cancer cells. Statistically, I had an 80 per cent chance that the cancer would return. An operation would improve this by 10 per cent. The harsh reality was that most bowel cancers did return and more people died of bowel cancer than survived.

I was faced with a choice, to have a life-changing, irreversible operation and slightly improve my chances of the cancer not returning, or opt to wait a few months, have another scan and reassess the state of play. If the cancer was still active, it would grow and be visible on the scans. For the time being, I could avoid drastic surgery that might not solve the problem anyway. Yet there was a risk in the 'wait and see' approach, that the cancer could spread. It had spread into the lymph system once and could do so again. While the weight of medical opinion suggested I should have the operation, my surgeon understood that there was a quality of life issue involved and accepted my choice not to have the operation.

But my choice was based on more than 'wait and see'. It was based on a growing conviction that God had spoken. An operation was not necessary because God had said the cancer was over. I walked away from my first hospital appointment after returning from Lagos knowing that I would have to return for more scans, but having decided not to have surgery. I decided to trust that I had heard from God, that it was over, and that at the next scan, there would be no sign of cancer. Each scan would prove that it was God's word for me that I had heard.

My situation has to be accepted by faith. Sometimes it feels as though I have two areas where I have to walk by faith. By faith, I accept that God is real, that he loves me and that I am saved. Also by faith, I accept that I no longer have bowel cancer and that the cancer will not return, that God has said it is over. I have to have faith that what I heard was from God and was true. I have moments of doubt. Only the other night I woke up in a cold sweat. What if it wasn't true and I was just kidding myself? The next scan would show an enlarged tumour and I would need more chemotherapy... Would I be able to face having another line fitted, more treatment pumped in?

At those times all I can do is cry out to God.

> Hear my cry, O God; listen to my prayer.
> From the ends of the earth I call to you,
> I call as my heart grows faint,
> Lead me to the rock that is higher than I.
>
> Psalm 61:1–2

What if I've got it all wrong? This book will make me look foolish, although only the most insensitive would rub my nose in it. I can't answer that one, but if I believe in an all-powerful God who is interested in me, there will be a point to all of it. I can live only in the here and now, but one day I will see the eternal perspective.

14. Blessed be the Name of the Lord[1]

The remainder of my sabbatical was spent writing this book, with more pleasant relaxing holidays fitted in. This jammy dodger returned to the 9 to 5 of the office one year after it all started; what a year!

Spending six weeks reliving the previous ten months was strange. At times I smiled as I remembered things done for me, the blessings I had received, the love shown. I was able to put together the threads of what God had said to me. I began to see how he had started to answer my early prayers, to use the situation for his glory, to change me, to make me into what he wanted. The work was by no means over but a lot had been accomplished. I was not the same person I was when it started. Lots remained, much has been remoulded, and lots new has been added.

At times I had to stop typing. Suddenly I could feel the emotions, almost as raw as when I first felt them. I cried again over the songs that meant so much. More than once I came close to throwing the laptop across the room, unable to cope with the feelings inside. I asked myself why was I doing this, why relive pain? To see its context, to see its value, to see its defeat. Somebody kindly said, you got through it once, you are strong enough to get through it again. They were right.

Will time wash away what has happened? Already I feel I'm forgetting things. Maybe this book will help me remember when I need to. I don't know what lies ahead, so many 'Don't knows', so many 'Cannot tells'. But this I know: I rest still and always will rest in the hands of my God.

* * *

Why have I chosen this song lyric? Those up to date with their music will have seen the link between the book title and this chapter title.

My heart will choose to say…blessed be the name of the Lord.

It's a choice. We choose to worship God, we choose to obey. It's easy in the good times, it's harder in the difficult times, but we can still choose to respond to everything with worship to God. It's an easy one to write but a harder one to do. I use the word 'worship' in a broader context than to refer purely to the times when we sing and pray in our church services. At times, my worship did involve song. I chose to sing words as a way of saying, 'This is what I believe, despite all the circumstances… Jesus commands my destiny.' Sometimes my act of worship was not to take out my frustrations on other people to make me feel better. Not turning my back on God and walking away from him when it seemed he wanted to take everything; this was an act of worship. It wasn't happy-clappy worship, putting on a brave face, smiling when I really wanted to cry. It was proclaiming that God was still sovereign, still in charge, still God, come what may. It's worship based on trust in who God is, not on what we feel. It hurts when we are ill, when God takes away. But when I chose to worship at these difficult times, I felt better for it. The pain didn't always go away but there was always a value.

Blessed be Your name in the land that is plentiful
Where your streams of abundance flow
Blessed be Your name

Blessed be Your name
When I'm found in the desert place
Though I walk through the wilderness
Blessed be Your name

Every blessing You pour out I'll turn back to praise
When the darkness closes in Lord still I will say
Blessed be the name of the Lord
Blessed be Your name

Blessed be Your name when the sun's shining down on me
When the world's all as it should be
Blessed be Your name

Blessed be Your name on the road marked with suffering
Though there's pain in the offering
Blessed be Your name

You give and take away
You give and take away
My heart will choose to say
Lord, blessed be Your name.

Note

1 Matt and Beth Redman, *Blessed Be Your Name* (© 2002 Thankyou Music)

15. I've had Questions, without Answers[1]

When I handed in the first draft of this book in September 2003 I had a nagging feeling that the story wasn't over, nor what I had written enough to explain what I believed God had done in my life. The story didn't seem over. This was confirmed by my own reaction to hearing my oncologist tentatively say that the cancer appeared to be in remission.

In September I returned to work, restored to full health. Over my four months off, I had been working away in the gym. My stamina levels had improved no end and I was feeling better than I had done for quite some time. I soon settled back into work, enjoying the challenge of a new role. There was lots to learn, lots to keep me busy. It was amazingly easy to forget the dramas of the previous twelve months. I was pleased I had taken time to write about it all as it began to feel like a distant dream.

The wake up call came in October, when it was time for the next set of scans. Suddenly it was a battle to believe that God had said the cancer was over as I was thrown back into the world of appointments, waiting rooms, gowns, blood tests, lying still in giant clanking machines. I was a patient again. I realised that fears I had thought were gone were in fact only partly hidden under the surface and easily came bubbling back up. Tests results showed no sign of active cancer, either at the site of the original tumour or in the swollen lymph gland. I tentatively asked if I was in remission. It was a very shaky reply; 'I think so.' My oncologist suggested that we wait a year before breaking open the champagne. While it was extremely good news, I was not yet in the clear. It was explained that it was common for cancers to respond well to treatment but to return within a short space of time. If this happened it would mean that the treatment would have been successful in reducing but not irradicating the cancer cells. A close eye would be kept on me.

'Remission' was a term that people could identify with, positive, upbeat, the first proof that the cancer was gone. It was time to celebrate, but I couldn't. My spirits dropped, not rose. I spent the weekend after receiving these results hidden away, feeling incredibly low. I didn't feel the crushing force I had a year before when first diagnosed, more an internal aching. I was confused by my own feelings. I had been given a prophecy that the cancer was gone, and here was the first proof. I'd written a book about all God had done for me. Was I not trusting in God, believing in what he had said? I couldn't bring myself to share these feelings with the people who kept coming to me saying how pleased they were, praising God for this evidence. I put on a smile, said hallelujah, and hated myself for not being the open, honest person I had fought to be throughout the treatment. I felt I was failing.

I had unfinished business. I had to work through some things. I wasn't healed instantly in answer to one person's prayer. I was given a prophecy that the cancer was over but God hadn't finished the work he wanted to do in me.

I thought I could walk away from the cancer and from the trauma of those twelve months but returning to hospital brought to the surface a fear that had to be faced. I have so struggled to write this section as I'm still trying to understand what happened myself and I don't know if I can fully explain it. Throughout much of my treatment I battled to believe that I actually had cancer and that what was happening to me was real. The threat of death over my life was genuine but it felt as if it hadn't sunk in to my rational mind. It had, however, sunk in somewhere because as I returned to the hospital in October I found I now feared cancer. This fear was cold and creeping. I'd think I was okay but suddenly it would be there. I'd head off to the hospital but it would be waiting for me at the entrance and I'd have to fight to make myself walk in. I would fight to listen during an appointment. While watching a storyline on TV where someone had cancer I'd feel the cold begin to grip. It was never an immobilising fear, but it came close.

I felt incredibly guilty. What right did I have to fear when God had said the cancer was gone? Was I looking back? In my mind I wasn't, I had decided to make a step of faith, to trust that God had spoken. I did not know where this fear came from.

It took some wise counsel to help me work through this. Over time I began to realise that I was human, maybe suffering from some form of post-traumatic stress. After all, I had been told quite often that I could die in the not too distant future. I learnt to stop feeling guilty about this fear but instead to offer it to God. Andy had been leading us in some meditations at church and I found one of them really helped. As the cold fear began to creep up I'd stop, hold my hands out in front of me and imagine the fear could be held in my hands. I'd ask God to take it, I offered it to him. Somehow this act led to the fear not overwhelming me. I was able to get up and carry on.

I had always struggled in my appointments to understand what was said to me and to remember it. I found I got worse, not better. I'd be focusing on just being at the appointment and not running away. I'd have no capacity left actually to listen. A friend helped me develop some coping strategies and to use some of my skills to tackle this. I'm an organised person and throughout my working life I'd had many opportunities to prepare agendas for meetings and then at the meeting gently ensure the key points were discussed. I transferred this skill. I prepared for medical appointments as if I was going to a business meeting. I prepared the questions I wanted answered and would ensure they were covered. I learnt to cope.

This may not sound very spiritual. Why are coping strategies needed when God has spoken? Certainly there has been no neat ending to my story. As much as I would like to wrap up this book with a list of evidence that I have been healed of cancer and my life completely transformed, I can't. The doctors will not validate my claim that the cancer is gone. Of course they are pleased that they can see no sign of active cancer as they scan me but I'm still a patient and the odds are still stacked against me. Medically speaking, there is still a greater chance that the cancer will return.

At first it did my head in trying to accept that people looked at me in two totally different ways. To some I was John Musgrave, the man amazingly healed of cancer with his whole life ahead of him, sunny and bright. To others I was John Musgrave the patient who had survived aggressive cancer but still had a long way to go before he was in the clear. This John's future was grey and uncertain. It hurt that there were people close to me in this second group who were unable to accept the definitive claim of the prophecy and who needed physical evidence. I couldn't provide it; nobody could. There was no doctor who could say 'He's healed.' No newspaper headlines, 'Man healed of cancer', no medical marvel stories on the local TV station. There was no definitive medical proof other than the fact that at that particular point there did not seem to be any cancer active and visible on the scans.

I have had to walk step by step, day by day, trusting in God, believing that he is in control, and that he has spoken. At times I have walked confidently and with conviction. Other times I have stumbled along, hardly daring to believe. I've fallen flat on my face, too scared to move at all. Yet it is my testimony that I know I have not walked this path on my own. God has been with me every step of the way. I don't know why he hasn't made it easier nor why I have had to learn to cope. Maybe this walk of faith is more valuable in the long run.

I do not want to be drawn into a discussion about the ministry of TB Joshua, the validity of his ministry, and if he truly gave me a prophecy from God but it seems that the issue must be faced. When I first considered going to Lagos I was aware of the questions many Christian leaders were asking about him, his church and his conduct. More recently these questions have begun to be asked outside of the Christian arena in the national media. The Channel 4 documentary *Is God Black?* visited the church and was scathing in its comments, particularly of the cultish behaviour of TB Joshua's disciples who appeared to be indoctrinated and to be worshipping him. I felt the programme made no allowances for African culture and viewed events in the church through a very analytical Western viewpoint. I also felt that the programme had a set agenda that had little to do with the actual life and work of those visited, and certainly nothing to do with the colour of God.

However, I shared the same concerns about how TB Joshua's disciples spoke of him and how they didn't seem to engage with the outside world. I too felt that he did not answer the questions put to him directly. I found the way they operated at the church to be bizarre. Yet I also saw a man who did everything in the name of Jesus, who continually said that it was not he who healed but God. I did not see a man milking his vast congregation for his own financial gain. I saw a man who held a very hard line on what constituted sin, a line way higher than that held by many in the UK.

As part of my walk of faith I have had to ask some difficult questions, and yes, the TV documentary did shake me. Did I really trust this man? But it was the wrong question. I had not placed my trust in TB Joshua, the validity of his ministry or his conduct. One year to the day I received the prophecy I was walking on a lovely wide beach in France as the sun set. As I looked back over the past year I realised that my trust was not based on the prophecy, nor the person who was the messenger. My trust was placed in God. He would not let me be deceived. He would not play games. He could be trusted. I couldn't tie up all the loose ends, tidy up the story, but I knew I trusted him with my future.

I heard the song I have chosen for this chapter while coming to terms with my post-prophecy life and it has helped me realise that some of our questions will not be answered. Where we may seek answers, we may have to make statements of faith, returning to what we know of God:

> I've had questions, without answers
> I've known sorrow, I have known pain
> But there's one thing that I'll cling to
> You are faithful, Jesus, You're true

When hope is lost I'll call You Saviour
When pain surrounds, I'll call You healer
When silence falls, You'll be the song within my heart
In the lone hour of my sorrow
Through the darkest night of my soul
You surround me and sustain me
My defender, forever more

I will praise You, I will praise You
When the tears fall, still I will sing to You
I will praise You, Jesus, praise You
Through the suffering still I will sing

When the laughter fails to comfort
When my heart aches Lord 'are You there?'
When confusion is all around me
And darkness is my closest friend

Still I will praise You
Jesus praise You.

Note

1 Tim Hughes, *I've Had Questions (When The Tears Fall)* (© 2003 Thankyou Music)

16. No one whose Hope is in You Will Ever be Put to Shame[1]

In December 2003 I had an endoscopy test, an unpleasant experience where a camera is fed through the bowel. The sides of the bowel wall can be clearly seen and polyps inspected. As I was leaving the ward, the nurse said that he had seen a lump on the bowel wall. I didn't panic as I knew there was still the scar tissue at the sight of the original tumour. However, I did have a few weeks with the nagging thought that something could be wrong. I also had another scan, the aim of which was to see if there was any sign of cancer anywhere else in the body. I was given the results of the test over the phone but I misunderstood the 'all clear' given. I thought they were referring to both the endoscopy and the CT scan results. When they said 'all clear' they were referring to the CT scan, stating that there was no evidence of cancer in any other part of my body.

With the Christmas holidays and then a mix up with appointments it wasn't until February that I was called in to see my surgeon.

I knew something was wrong the moment I stepped into my surgeon's office. The Macmillan nurse was there, and various others. It was too large a crowd for a routine check-up. They showed me a picture that had been taken during the endoscopy. There was clearly a growth on the bowel wall and it didn't look good. They explained that they needed to do a biopsy but they suspected it to be malignant. If it was, it was time to have the dreaded operation to remove my bowel.

It was hard to argue with a picture, in fact it was the first time I had ever been shown anything that I could identify as a tumour. Before, I just had to accept there was something there that shouldn't be. I could never identify anything on the scans they showed me. But this lump did not look good.

Satan is portrayed in Mel Gibson's film *The Passion* as an asexual being, quietly present in the background taunting Jesus throughout the torture scenes. He is not a little red devil with horns and a prong. Far more sinisterly, he whispers in Jesus' ear: 'Did God really say?' I walked out of the hospital to that taunt in my ear; 'Did God really say?'

It had been easier to believe I no longer had cancer, surrounded by people who accepted what had been said to me in Lagos. When the scan results came back all clear and everybody rejoiced, there seemed to be medical proof to back up the bold claim 'It is finished.' It was much harder faced with a medical team fearing that the inevitable had happened, a year after treatment the tumour had recovered and returned. I felt as if the ground under my feet was shaking.

For a couple of days I was in a daze. My mind raced down various paths. God hadn't spoken in Lagos, the cancer wasn't gone, I was going to die. Maybe I wouldn't die but I was going to have to face this operation, learn to live with a colostomy bag. This was a test, God was testing me. Did I trust him enough to say that the doctors were wrong? So many chains of thought surrounded by the taunt, 'Did God really say?'

The scariest thought which dominated was that God had said the cancer was over, but he had also said to take sin seriously and pursue righteousness. I realised again, to my shame, that I hadn't pursued righteousness. I'd come back from Lagos on a high, with great intentions but again let my guard slip. Had I stepped out from under God's protection, had my sin meant I was no longer protected from the cancer returning? Had I brought this upon myself?

Despite these thoughts I was not thrown back a year and a half into the turmoil felt when I was first diagnosed. I was not crushed, I did not do an awful lot of crying. I had learnt some lessons and now was the time to put some things into practice. I had said, not only said but written in this book, that my destiny lay in God's hands. Even death by cancer could not separate me from him. I was his, he was mine. If I had totally misunderstood what had happened in Lagos, or had been deceived, and the cancer was not gone, he was still in control. I still did not know how my own sin and my own sickness were linked but I knew that the Holy Spirit didn't convict us of sin so that we could wallow in guilt. He brought conviction to lead us to repentance. So it was back to Andy for round two of the confessions. What needed to be said was said and I truly repented. I still wondered if I had brought this on myself but felt all I could do was repent. At church a few days later someone came to me and gave me a verse:

> For his anger lasts only a moment,
> but his favour lasts a lifetime;
> weeping may remain for a night,
> but rejoicing comes in the morning.
>
> Psalm 30:5

I cried then, couldn't stop myself. I realised that it didn't matter if my sin meant the cancer could return. I had been forgiven, I felt forgiven. If God was angry at my sin, he had accepted my repentance. Grace again, so amazing, so totally undeserved.

I was given this verse at the end of a morning church service where George had been baptised. I helped Andy baptise her. It was a challenge to sing one of the songs she chose for the service, particularly the second verse:

> To you O Lord, I lift up my soul
> In you I trust, O my God.
> Do not let me be put to shame
> Nor let my enemies triumph over me.
>
> No one whose hope is in you
> Will ever be put to shame
> That's why my eyes are on you, O Lord.
> Surround me, defend me,
> O, how I need you.
> To you I lift up my soul.

This song, based on Psalm 25, encapsulated a cry from within me, a cry to God for help. Not just help to survive, but help to keep trusting in him when his very words to me, the centre of the testimony of what God had done for me, seemed to be under attack. All I had said, all I had written would appear foolish, meaningless, shameful, if all that happened was that the cancer returned as the doctors expected. Sometimes I'm able to sing such songs with conviction, knowing the words to be true. This time I had to sing them believing them to be true despite the circumstances, to sing them in faith.

It felt as if Satan wanted to rob me of my testimony, to shame me. To shout out: 'See, God never said anything to him, It isn't finished.' Ultimately he wanted to shame God. It felt right to stand and say 'No' and to keep on trusting despite the circumstances.

To say I battled through the week that followed my doctor's appointment would be an understatement. I felt as if I was Gandalf in *The Fellowship of The Rings,* facing a large evil creature and shouting 'You shall not pass' as the bricks of the bridge beneath fell away. Yet I knew, maybe as Gandalf knew on that bridge, that it would be better to stand my ground and fight, risking destruction, than to turn and run. I believe Satan wanted me to give in, to get angry with God, to curse him and to give up believing that God controlled my destiny. I stood my ground. Oh, I trembled as I stood, wobbled and fell over but I got up again and stood my ground.

I wasn't alone. Again people prayed for me. Some felt strongly that the lump was not cancer and prayed that it would soon be proved to be nothing more than a lump. Others believed that they should pray that the promise God had made would be honoured. What was significant to me was that many people refused to accept that God was not in full control of the situation. At the first big test, people who prayed and supported me did not turn and say, 'Oh well, we got it wrong, God didn't speak.' Rather, they believed God had spoken and got on their knees and said, 'God, be glorified in this situation.' It was a testing time for more people than just me but it led to some powerful praying.

While others were convinced that this could not be cancer returning, I was not so sure. I dealt with the issue of sin and did my best to turn to God, not away from him. It felt right to say 'Come what may, I will not stop believing in God, not stop worshipping him, nor stop trusting him.' I was inspired by the story of Shadrach, Meshach and Abednego found in the book of Daniel. Faced with the threat of death in a furnace if they didn't worship an idol, they stood their ground. They believed God could save them and stated so clearly. However, they acknowledged that God could choose not to save them. They could die, but still they would not give in:

> If we are thrown into the blazing furnace, the God
> we serve is able to save us from it, and he will rescue us
> from your hands, O king. But even if he does not, we
> want you to know, O king, that we will not serve your
> gods or worship the image of gold you have set up.
> Daniel 3:17–18

The issue was not whether God would or wouldn't save them, it was whether they would obey God. The issue for me was not would God save me from dying of cancer, but would I refuse to reject him and still trust him. I chose to trust him, despite the circumstances. To say to Satan, even if I die of cancer, I will not reject my God.

I do not write this to boast. I include this bit because I believe that everybody's faith is tested by the circumstances they find themselves in. To me, Christianity is not about trusting in God because by doing so he makes our life easier, more comfortable and content. I believe Christianity is about trusting in God regardless of our circumstances; believing he is there, believing the things he says about himself and about us found in the Bible, and worshipping him no matter what. Nor did I include this bit because I am doubting what God has said. I believe the cancer is gone. At times I doubt but each day I do my best to trust that God spoke to me, step by step to believe his word. Sometimes I still have to face the fear of cancer and death and it shakes me to the bone. However, I realise now that my faith must be based on more than the state of my health. I must accept God and trust in him regardless of what happens.

* * *

My heart is spoken for[2]

On the first Saturday morning after my appointment I got out my notebook, my draft of this book, all the cards people had sent me and my Bible. I spent the morning going over the things I had learnt. I read the Bible passages, I listened to the songs. It was all still true, it all still applied. God was still my rock, he still shone, nothing could separate me from him. I could still trust in his faithfulness.

I realised again that ultimately it didn't matter if cancer claimed my life. I was God's and he was mine and nothing could separate us. In this knowledge I found amazing freedom. Fears could still rise up but I could face them with truth. Satan could come and whisper, 'Did God say?', and I could answer, 'Yes, he did.'

I could not only tell him he couldn't pass, I could tell him that he couldn't have me at all. I was spoken for:

> Take this world from me, I don't need it any more.
> I am finally free,
> My heart is spoken for
>
> Covered by a love divine
> Child of the risen Lord
> To hear you say 'This one's mine'
> My heart is spoken for.

A few days later my surgeon removed the lump and tests showed it to be benign. I'm still pondering why God allowed this mini cancer scare but I can see the value of the test for my life, and for others who choose to pray with me. I don't know if I will have to go through similar scares again, whether I am going to have to keep on fighting to take hold of what God has said and done. My last PET scan showed no sign of cancer and the swollen lymph gland could not be seen. All clear and free to go until the next test. But God has continued to use these experiences to mould me, to refine my faith, and to show me he loves me. I have also had the pleasure of seeing how my story has encouraged others in their Christian walk. I was shown this verse recently:

> They overcame him by the blood of the Lamb
> and by the word of their testimony.

Revelation 12:11

I have seen how my testimony, when shared with others, has helped some people in their fight. What I have written is an honest account of how God worked in my life during a particular segment of my journey. It's not a neat story and for me it isn't finished, not by a long shot, but I pray it will encourage others regardless of the circumstances of their lives.

Notes

1 Graham Kendrick, *To You Oh Lord* (© 1997 Make Way Music. International copyright secured. All rights reserved. Used by permission)

2 Bart Millard, Nathan Cochran, Mike Scheucher, Robby Shaffer, Pete Kipley, *My Heart Is Spoken For* (© 2002 Simpleville Music/administered by Copycare)

Addresses of copyright holders

Buck Music Ltd., 11 Uxbridge Street, London W8 7TQ.

CopyCare, P.O. Box 77, Hailsham, East Sussex, BN27 3EF. music@copycare.com

Make Way Music UK, P.O. Box 263, Croydon, Surrey, CR9 5AP.

Sovereign Music UK, P.O. Box 356, Leighton Buzzard, Bedfordshire, LU7 8WP. sovereignmusic@aol.com

Til Dawn Music, CA, USA
Warner/Chappell North America, London, W6 8BS
Reproduced by permission of International Music Publications Ltd. All rights reserved.

Thank you Music Adm. by worshiptogether.com/org excl. UK. Europe, adm. by Kingsway Music tym@kingsway.co.uk. Used by permission

EMI Music Publishing Ltd. London WC2H 0QY

Grace Choices

by Jeff Lucas

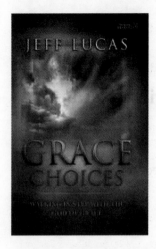

'Grace is the jewel we possessed all along but had seemingly mislaid. Jeff Lucas helps us find it, polish, treasure it.'

Rob Parsons, Care for the Family

The grace of God – his undeserved love and favour towards you – presents you with choices. Will you choose to see God through the lens of grace? Will you opt to see yourself – and others – the same way? Do you really believe in his free forgiveness towards others?

In this powerful book, Jeff Lucas unpacks grace in its fullness and shows how, if you choose, grace can work through you and in you to transform your relationships, your church and your life. With his trademark mix of insight, humour and passion, this book will show you how to take the grace God offers you as you decide to change your world.

'A powerful and deeply insightful contribution to our understanding of Divine Grace. It kept me enthralled to the very last word.'
Andy Hawthorne, The Message Trust

'I wholeheartedly recommend *Grace Choices*. Jeff Lucas is my trusted friend; he's honest, thoughtful, thought-provoking and very funny, but most importantly he loves God – all of which mean that this book is a wonderful travel guide for the adventurous.'
Selwyn Hughes, author of *Every Day with Jesus*

'Jeff Lucas is an absolute gift to the church…a brilliant, witty and challenging book.'
Steve Chalke MBE, Oasis Trust

Jeff is teaching pastor at Timberline Church, Fort Collins, Colorado in the USA; part of the Spring Harvest leadership team and a hugely popular international speaker and teacher.

ISBN: 1-85078-554-6

Available from your local Christian bookshop or www.WesleyOwen.com

Lift the Label

by David Westlake and Esther Stansfield

Lift the Label is a wake-up call to connect our faith in God with our everyday lifestyle choices. It reveals the hidden faces, and tells the unheard stories, of people we come into contact with every day, without even realising it – the people who make our food and clothes.

Taking a journey into the bible to expose western Christianity's great blind spot, *Lift the Label* uncovers how much the poor matter to God. It challenges us to change our consumer choices to reflect His heart for justice.

Written to inspire and empower, this book contains creative and practical ways to shop differently. It explains fair trade and provides a much-needed directory of ethically minded shops, to help us have a positive impact on our global neighbours when we hit the high street.

The daily decisions we make with our money can be life changing for the poor.

How can *your* lifestyle make a difference?

> 'Incisive, relevant, practical and vital teaching. I highly commend it.'
> Mike Pilavachi, Soul Survivor

> 'Too often Christians struggle about their lifestyle – how to be distinctively Christian in a consumer society, and feel powerless about global injustice – what possible difference could I make? This splendidly practical book provides answers to both questions. Highly recommended!'
> Graham Cray, Bishop of Maidstone

ISBN: 1-85078-572-4

Available from your local Christian bookshop or www.WesleyOwen.com

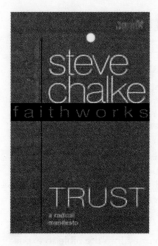

Trust: a Radical Manifesto

Steve Chalke and Anthony Watkis

There are countless commentaries on the reasons for the erosion of trust in society today. The government, the media, the royal family, the church, the police, the law lords, and many more have tumbled from their pedestals. But, rather than a catalogue of reasons for failure this is a manual for reconstruction. Steve Chalke examines practical ways through which trust can be built in 21st century society and asks hard questions of government and church as they both strive to become more trusted by the public and each other.

'Timely, thought provoking and debate-inducing. I commend it to you as a tool for change.'

Joel Edwards, Evangelical Alliance

'This book shows how we need to work together to repair the damage caused in the last few decades by the loss of trust.'

Andy Reed MP, Labour

'Steve's book will inspire us all.'

Caroline Spelman MP, Conservative

'Steve Chalke provides a refreshing alternative to the lazy cynicism which says that engaging with the political world is a waste of time…It is time to take on the cynics, and this book provides us with a road map.'

Steve Webb MP, Liberal Democrat

Steve Chalke MBE is the founder of Oasis Global and the Faithworks Movement as well as an author, broadcaster, speaker and the senior minister of the church.co.uk centre, Waterloo.

Anthony Watkis is a graduate of The London School of Theology. He is a professional writer and works with Oasis UK.

ISBN: 1-85078-586-4

Available from your local Christian bookshop or www.WesleyOwen.com